Praise for *Solar Dividends*

Robert Stayton has a wonderful new idea in this book. For years, some visionary people have been promoting a universal basic income, but they have been defeated by the problem of financing: who will pay for it? Stayton has the answer. The sun belongs to us all, and solar energy will pay for it. It is an idea worth very broad consideration.

—John Isbister, Professor of Economics Ryerson University

Stopping climate change and enacting a universal basic income may seem like very different goals, but Robert Stayton presents a compelling case for how we can achieve both together. *Solar Dividends* is a big idea we should be seriously discussing as we take on the complex challenges of the 21st century.

—Jim Pugh, Co-Founder of Universal Income Project

Climate change and income security are the two great challenges facing our world, with the impact of global warming and new technology. This book offers a bold and original way to link solutions to both - massive investment in solar energy and unconditional Basic Incomes for all. The argument for how the former could, over the present century, come to finance the latter, is detailed, imaginative and far-sighted.

—Bill Jordan, author of *Authoritarianism and How to Counter It.*

The agricultural revolution, the industrial revolution, and the digital revolution all led to a small number of people becoming immensely wealthy. Robert Stayton's plan would make sure that the solar revolution produces the opposite — a fairer, more equitable society.

—Denis Hayes, Founder of the Earth Day Network

Robert Stayton has made a great proposal for basic income which is based on a dividend from activity which we want to encourage (as opposed to carbon dividends from what we need to discourage), and is scalable to different communities. It should be read by all interested in basic income and in protecting the environment.

—Barb Jacobson, Co-ordinator of Basic Income UK

There have been many ideas on how to finance a basic income for everyone, and solve the climate crisis on planet Earth. But these have traditionally been seen as separate. Why not put them together? That is exactly what Robert Stayton has done: written a compelling argument for using solar energy to produce a steady flow of income, and then distribute it unconditionally for all people. That should work to get humanity off the fossil fuel addiction for good, and provide the dignity and freedom so many people desperately need today.

—André Coelho, Chief Editor of Basic Income News

A vital idea that has potential to disrupt the way we imagine providing both energy and decent livelihoods.

—Dr. Katherine Trebeck, Policy & Knowledge Lead,
Wellbeing Economy Alliance

Stayton's proposal is brilliantly straightforward yet thoroughly considered. He argues persuasively for the implementation of a solar-energy-based unconditional basic income for all human beings. This potentially world-changing book must find its way into the hands of activists, community leaders, policymakers, and government officials around the globe—the sooner, the better.

—Sarah Juniper Rabkin, writer, editor, and retired UC
Santa Cruz instructor in environmental studies

Solar Dividends

HOW SOLAR ENERGY CAN GENERATE A
BASIC INCOME FOR EVERYONE ON EARTH

Robert Stayton

Sandstone
PUBLISHING

Sandstone Publishing
PO Box 2911 Santa Cruz, CA 95063
info@sandstonepublishing.com
www.sandstonepublishing.com

ISBN 978-0-9904792-3-9 (Print edition)
ISBN 978-0-9904792-4-6 (Kindle edition)
ISBN 978-0-9904792-5-3 (EPUB edition)

Library of Congress Control Number: 2019903995
BISAC Subject Code: SOC037000 SOCIAL SCIENCE / Future Studies
BISAC Subject Code: POL068000 POLITICAL SCIENCE / Public Policy / Energy Policy
BISAC Subject Code: US070040 BUSINESS & ECONOMICS / Industries / Energy

Contents

A New Approach

No one owns the sun. This simple and obvious fact has been true since humans invented the concept of ownership. Before now, no one paid attention to this fact, because the idea of anyone owning something as big and powerful as the sun seems absurd.

Now this fact has emerged from obscurity to become vitally important for the survival of modern civilization. That's because humanity has embarked on a dramatic shift in the most fundamental resource that we use—energy. We are witnessing a historic shift from fossil fuels to renewable energy, and we have an unprecedented opportunity to ensure that this time everyone can benefit from the energy that runs our civilization.

Humans built modern society over the last two hundred years by burning fossil fuels to mine minerals, power our factories, produce our food, and transport our goods. But now the carbon dioxide released over two centuries of burning carbon-based fuels has accumulated in our atmosphere to levels not seen for three million years, triggering climate change and ocean acidification. The effects of these changes threaten to wreck human habitats, agriculture, and the world economy, putting vast numbers of people at risk.

"Even as we witness devastating climate impacts causing havoc across the world, we are still not doing enough, nor moving fast enough, to prevent irreversible and catastrophic climate disruption. For many people, regions [and] even countries, this is already a matter of life and death."

This ominous warning came from United Nations Secretary-General António Guterres as international leaders convened in Poland in December 2018 for the COP24 conference on global warming.[1]

He sounded the alarm because the first twenty-three annual COP climate summits, starting with COP1 in 1995, saw each in turn fail to arrest world carbon emissions, which continue to grow beyond all targeted limits. Despite his warning, a headline published at the end of the conference sang the same tired refrain: "COP24: Countries struggle to muster political will to tackle climate crisis."[2]

Why so little progress? Because just a few people, corporations, and nations own fossil fuels, and those owners resist efforts to convert from fossil fuels to clean renewable energy. If we do convert, then their reserves become worthless. So they use their enormous energy wealth to fund think tanks to obscure the science of climate change, pay lobbyists to pressure politicians to delay actions, and support media mavens to sow doubt about renewable energy.[3]

Need proof that energy interests are powerful? At a time when we should be cutting back on fossil fuels, the US paid $649 billion in direct and indirect subsidies to coal, oil, and gas interests in 2015, according to the International Monetary Fund.[4] That's more than the entire US military budget for 2015 ($599 billion). Worldwide, fossil fuel subsides totaled $5.3 trillion, or 6.5% of global GDP. It takes considerable clout to get nations who say they are trying to control carbon emissions to instead provide that much support for maintaining those emissions.

If catastrophic climate change doesn't motivate nations to overcome the resistance from fossil fuel interests, we should stop beating our heads against the wall, step back, and approach the problem from a different angle. That's what this book does. Instead of confronting global warming head-on, it advances an original solution to economic insecurity, and that solution carries with it an automatic side effect of addressing climate change.

This solution develops from a novel idea—that we set up every person on the planet with a big section of solar panels, sell the electricity the panels generate, and give the money to the person as "solar dividends" for life.

This solution derives from four incontestable facts:

- **Solar energy is inexhaustible.** Our sun has been delivering energy to Earth for five billion years, and will continue for another five billion years.
- **Solar energy is available all over the world.** Solar energy falls on all inhabited parts of the globe, more so in some places than others.
- **Solar energy has economic value.** When photovoltaic panels convert the sun's rays to electricity, that electricity can be sold for cash.
- **No one owns the sun.**

Since no one owns the sun, it's fair to say that everyone has a right to a share of solar energy, because anyone can collect solar energy and put it to use. At this point our laws have not yet defined this as a legal right, nor has the United Nations declared it as a human right. It's more of a natural right, equivalent to your right to breathe in the air from the atmosphere we all share.

This book takes that notion a step further by turning that natural right into a practical program, showing how we can make a better world by helping everyone to collect their share of solar energy.

There is certainly enough sun to go around. Every five days the sun delivers to Earth the energy equivalent to all the fossil fuel reserves in the world. Harvesting just one part in 6,000 of the solar energy hitting our planet would replace all the energy we use worldwide today. And the most important feature of solar energy that distinguishes it from fossil fuels is that it won't run out, so this will be the last energy transition we need to make.

In the twenty-first century, the best way to harvest that solar energy is with photovoltaic (PV) panels. PV panels sit silently in the sun and generate electricity that feeds into the electric grid to power our modern world. Because people pay for that electricity, solar panels can generate money, day after day, year after year. We can distribute that money as solar dividends, and with enough panels we can generate solar dividends for everyone on Earth.

Distributing money is easier than distributing solar panels. Giving everyone solar panels to generate their own electricity might seem like a good idea, but it would not be fair. Those that don't own property to put them on would find the panels to be useless. Even those with property may not have suitable space to install solar panels, or they may have poor access to sunlight because of trees and buildings. Community solar farms put panels on leased land in the best sunny locations and distribute the benefits as money instead of electricity.

We could largely eliminate poverty because the money the panels generate becomes a minimum basic income for each person. We would do that to reverse the growing economic disparity in the world, lift everyone out of deep poverty, and erect a stable economic floor on which people can build lives as jobs disappear into robotics and artificial intelligence.

When we reach the stage where we've installed enough panels to cover everyone, the combined electrical power of those panels will generate enough energy to replace fossil fuels almost entirely. As we stop burning fossil fuels, carbon emissions will drop, and we can halt the march toward catastrophic global warming. At that point, we will be running on sustainable and clean energy sources that can carry humanity far into the future.

This new approach transforms the effort. Instead of struggling against climate change, we work to secure the economic welfare of every person. The focus shifts from invisible carbon dioxide to real people, and the problem scales down from global to individual. We strive to save people, not the world, but in the end the world gets saved too.

So by tackling the problem of poverty, we deal with the problem of climate change. That's how we approach climate change from a different angle.

We sidestep the label of "utopian dream" by building this project with real hardware in the form of solar panels and generating real money that people can spend. If we install enough of this hardware and distribute the benefits as described in this book, then we will go a long way toward solving three of the world's biggest and most intractable problems: global poverty, global warming, and global energy supply.

The program pays for itself from the revenue generated by the solar panels themselves. The money first pays off the installation costs and then pays for the ongoing solar dividends. Because solar energy arrives endlessly, the money the panels generate for each person flows endlessly. If the panels are maintained and replaced as needed, the money can flow for a lifetime, from birth to death.

The plan reaches unprecedented breadth by including everyone. Every person living on Planet Earth would be eligible. Never has an economic plan encompassed everyone. We can do that because every nation on the planet gets a share of solar energy.

And because the idea includes everyone, it creates a force of unity among all people. Unlike fossil fuels, solar energy is a common resource we can all share. Solar dividends will be a positive thing whose benefits all people receive, something we can promote and defend because of all the good they do.

Solar dividends are for you, your children, your grandchildren, and all of your descendants. If you help build this idea into reality, you'll create a legacy that connects you to all of your succeeding generations. Solar dividends offer a path of hope for our future.

You may think this sounds too good to be true. You might understand the basic idea, but can't yet see how it would work in our present world. This book explains how we can do it, starting from where we are now.

My program is easy to grasp, but not easy to carry out. In order for this idea to succeed, several threads have to work together. Rather than show you one thread at a time, let me first describe the whole tapestry they weave, so you get a picture of where we are going. In Part A, I'll present to you a vision of the future based on the most straightforward approach for creating solar dividends. Then in Part B, I'll switch to the present and examine that approach in more detail to see how we can reach that future. I'll also present alternative approaches in case the primary one meets too much political resistance, or if alternatives might work better in different locations.

Much of the interesting technology described in Part A is already under development, as documented in the endnotes. You may still have some questions after reading Part A, but you'll find many answers in Part B. If you are impatient to get to the nuts and bolts, you can skip ahead and read Part B first.

A Vision of the Future

CHAPTER 1

The World is Still Functioning in 2099

THE YEAR IS 2099, and the world is positioning itself to transition from the old 21st century into the new 22nd century. Now is a time to reflect on the past and anticipate the future.

I'm forty-nine years old, and I'm optimistic when I regard that future. My optimism sharply contrasts with the pessimism my grandparents expressed as they grew up in the early decades of the 21st century. Back then, they faced three daunting worldwide problems: economic inequality on the scale of ancient Rome, a vital energy source on the verge of failure, and runaway global warming.

All three problems were growing unchecked and pushing the world toward the collapse of modern society. Government officials often acknowledged the three problems, but couldn't cope with any of them. Economic structures of the day resisted change. Those three problems spanned the globe, but no worldwide political body had enough power to overcome the resistance.

Our civilization continued to drift toward cliff edges in three directions. My grandparents felt helpless because all the politicians, academics, and activists in the world couldn't slow their slide into disaster. They wondered what ordinary people might do about those looming worldwide catastrophes.

Yet civilization survived and modern society still functions in 2099. A happenstance combined with intent ushered humanity through the dangerous times.

The happenstance was the Great Energy Crisis in 2025 which boosted energy prices and focused everyone's attention on the changing economics of energy. That crisis appeared apocalyptic until humanity realized that we could use those higher energy prices to make improvements. That led to the intent part, and it worked.

The actions taken during the 21st century resulted in a new economic order, one that has sustained us to the present, and one that can continue to sustain us into the future. Thankfully, the changes weren't imposed by violent revolution or strong-arm dictators, but by an incremental and peaceful transformation of the energy foundation supporting our world economy.

I can best describe it by telling you the story of one typical increment of that change—my story.

CHAPTER 2

My Story

MY ECONOMIC STORY STARTS just before I was born in
2050. When my parents were young and preparing the baby
room for my birth, they also took the extra step of registering
me for my standard solar energy array.

They contacted their local community solar cooperative,
which was installing photovoltaic panels on solar farms in various locations inside and outside our city. My expectant father
and pregnant mother signed me up for a ten-kilowatt section of
PV panels at the Cloverfield Solar Farm.

Here's how it worked. My young parents didn't have the
money to buy the panels outright, but they didn't need to.
When they signed me up, the co-op borrowed the money to
install the panels with a government-guaranteed loan. The
guarantee brought with it government regulation and inspection to prevent fraud.

My parents never had to make payments on that loan. After
the co-op installed and connected the PV panels on the solar
farm, the co-op sold the electricity to the local electric utility
grid. The $1,000 per month the co-op received from the utility

company covered the loan payments. The electricity revenue paid back my solar loan by the time I was four years old.

On the day of final payoff, something magical happened: the co-op threw a switch, and the money that had been flowing to the bank to pay the loan instead started flowing into my personal co-op savings account. The money generated by my section of panels accrued to me, minus a small percentage kept by the co-op for maintenance and management.

While I was growing up, between the ages of four and eighteen, the co-op deposited those solar dividends into my personal Solar Fund. The co-op maintained that member account to accumulate the cash that my panels generated. At eighteen, my Solar Fund held about $200,000 in accumulated solar dividends and interest.[1]

I remember my parents taking me to visit my panels on the solar farm. I saw flat panels on racks held up by poles spread over pasture land. The motorized racks slowly turned to always face the sun, like sunflowers. The co-op manager explained that my panels were semitransparent, tuned to absorb orange, yellow and green wavelengths of sunlight to generate electricity, while transparent to the red and blue wavelengths that plants needed for photosynthesis.[2] By passing those wavelengths through, the grass could still grow under the panels as if the panels weren't there. I remember seeing the purple-colored sun as I looked up through the panels because of the differential filtering of the light.

Dairy cows grazed on the grass growing underneath the panels. I think they appreciated the partial shade on hot days and the shelter on rainy days. The semitransparent panels allowed the co-op to lease the overhead space at a low price, because the land kept its original use for the farmer. That made the arrangement worthwhile for the farmer who continued to pasture her cows while receiving monthly solar lease payments. The land itself benefited from the partial shade, which reduced water evaporation, encouraging the grass to grow lusher for the cows.[3]

I listened to the speech about how my panels generated clean electricity to solve the world's carbon emissions problem. I also remember that the visit was a bit boring. The panels just sat there in the sun and generated electricity invisible to me and consumed by someone far away. If you've seen one solar panel, you've seen them all.

I remember one part of the talk: that humans have *always* relied on energy from the sun to survive and grow. We started by burning wood that sunlight grew, progressed through the fossil fuels created by ancient sunlight, and on to the direct solar and wind systems that power our society today. We've always used solar energy, either directly or indirectly, and we always will. My panels represent my piece of that history and future.

While I was still a child, the co-op classified me as a junior member. The co-op still held my solar panels in my name, and I learned how the co-op worked, but I didn't yet have co-op voting rights. My mother served as a proxy member and voted on my behalf on any co-op issues that came before members. At the age of eighteen I graduated to full co-op membership, taking over the voting rights from my mother.

At eighteen another magical change occurred: the co-op threw a second switch, and the solar money that had been flowing into my co-op savings fund instead flowed directly into my checking account. Every month from the age of eighteen to my current age of forty-nine, I saw a $1,000 electronic deposit from the co-op appear in my bank account. As long as the co-op maintains the equipment, I will continue to receive payments.

The $1,000 comes from selling the 13,000 kilowatt-hours (kwh) of electricity per year that my ten-kilowatt PV array generates. The co-op sells it to the local utility for $.95 per kwh, and the co-op keeps $.02 per kwh for operating expenses, leaving me with $.93 per kwh. That generates $12,000 for the year, which the co-op divides into twelve payments. So I get a $1,000 solar dividend appearing in my bank account every month.

The money arrives with no strings attached regarding how I use it. It is my personal responsibility to manage my own solar dividends, based on the guidance provided by my parents and the co-op.

I call them my panels, but I don't actually own them. The co-op retains ownership of the hardware. What I'm granted is the right to the solar dividends the panels generate. I can't sell my panels because I don't own them. I can't mortgage my future solar dividends either, as that would violate co-op rules and cause me to lose my dividends.

I'm glad I don't own the panels, as my life would be more complicated if I did. If I moved away, I couldn't easily take them with me, and my new home might not be suitable to mount them. Since I derive only money from the panels (someone else uses the energy), the panels can stay where they are and the co-op can wire the money to me wherever I go.

Why would the co-op be so generous with me? It's not. I'm a member of a co-op whose stated purpose in its charter is to deliver solar dividends to members. So the co-op is not being generous, it's fulfilling its purpose. Co-ops differ from corporations because they optimize benefits to members, not to shareholders.

After graduating from high school, I had a nest egg in my Solar Fund and a small income showing up on my bank statement every month, so I was ready to start my adult life. Like many of my peers, I chose to go to college. Education had grown in importance because paid jobs for uneducated people were becoming scarce. Automation was continuing to take over most physical work and menial tasks, so there wasn't much future in being a laborer.

My solar dividends made it much easier to attend college. I paid my expenses with my monthly dividends, living the frugal life of a student in a shared household. If need be, I had access to my Solar Fund for emergencies. But I tried to preserve that fund, as I anticipated buying a house or starting a business after graduation.

Tuition at most state colleges is free, for two reasons. The first is that research showed how a more highly educated population was more productive, prosperous, and happy, so the investment in education improved society in many ways.

The second reason is solar dividends freed up some money that formerly went to welfare programs. Welfare remained available for those who needed it, but solar dividends enabled a natural attrition off of welfare as people became more self-sufficient through the opportunities solar dividends provided. Governments converted part of the welfare savings into free tuition for state colleges, an investment to help keep people off of welfare.

After college, I took my first job, earning enough money to allow my monthly solar dividends to accumulate again in my Solar Fund. But my employer eliminated my job after four years. The world was continuing its transition to robotics and artificial intelligence, and the company automated my job out from under me.

After my layoff, I fell back on my solar dividends, living in a shared household again. I wanted to work because I preferred to live a lifestyle a cut above that which my basic solar dividends supported. I also derive personal satisfaction from doing worthwhile work and interacting with people.

I took a few classes to improve my qualifications, but paid jobs were scarce. It took a year of searching, but I finally found another job that satisfied me. Without the support of solar dividends, I would have been forced to accept any job. With those dividends I could take time to find a good job.

When I was twenty-five, my solar panels needed replacement after twenty-five years in the sun. Replacement costs were much lower than the original panels because of technological advances while I was growing up. The co-op paid for the replacements out of a fund they had built up for that purpose.

My replacement panels used the latest nano-antenna technology[4] with a fifty-year estimated lifetime, so the co-op will probably not need to replace them until I'm seventy-five. The replacements were also twice as efficient as the old panels. That freed up half the original panel area to support another co-op member.

At twenty-seven I got married, and my spouse and I merged our two solar incomes so we could rent our own apartment. We planned to use our joint Solar Funds to buy a house. Our intention was to start a family and enroll our own children in the solar dividend program because it was such a good experience for us. People joined not because they had to, but because it was valuable to their children. And it cost nothing to sign up.

A few of my friends took different paths, developing their literary, artistic or musical talents instead of working paid jobs. You could take time off, live cheaply, and write that great book or song that floated in the back of your mind. Some were financially successful in their creative efforts, and others lived on the basic support coming from their solar dividends, but no artists were literally starving.

Some people pursue socially beneficial but unpaid activities such as caring for their children or elder relatives, cleaning up the environment, or engaging in social activism. It can be immensely satisfying to put your time and energy into what you believe in.

You don't get rich on your solar dividends, so most people work to rise above the basic income. Solar dividends gave industrious individuals the means to develop their own businesses. While working regular jobs, they used their solar dividends to buy equipment and supplies, develop marketing materials, and hire help to set up their enterprises.

Some refrain from contributing to society, either from laziness or antisocial hostility, but that's their choice. Solar dividends grant freedom—freedom from government control of your life through welfare requirements, and freedom from odious and degrading jobs. As long as you don't harm others, no one objects because you are living on the income from your solar panels.

My parents are now retired and living on a combination of their solar dividends, Social Security, and the investments they made during their lifetimes. I soon must spend time providing more care and support for them in their old age, and I'll be able to do that with the flexibility granted by my solar dividends.

Now that I'm forty-nine and the kids are out of the house, I'm thinking of becoming an artisan woodcrafter. I'll use my Solar Fund to set up a shop and use my monthly dividends to support me during my startup. I expect to have a satisfying life of work creating beautiful and useful things, because life is not about being lazy but about expressing one's own vitality.

Part A: A Vision of the Future

CHAPTER 3

Solar for Everyone

THE SOLAR DIVIDEND PROGRAM worked so well to keep people out of poverty that co-ops set up solar dividend programs for adults who'd missed getting signed up at birth. Adults had to wait until their panels paid off their installation cost before solar dividends could start.

In 2076, when I was twenty-six, the world completed the build-out of solar for nearly everyone, all over the world. Almost every country had policies in place to help people get connected to solar dividends. Countries with many people living in extreme poverty in remote villages took longer, but eventually the programs excluded no one who wanted to take part. The effort wiped out most of the crushing poverty that had plagued civilizations for centuries.

Solar dividends have always been my economic safety net. My parents' actions at my birth in 2050 established a solid economic foundation for my life. No one tells me what to do or how to spend my money. I'm a self-reliant person free to contribute to society as I see fit.

And so is everyone else. Solar electricity proved to be an exceptional match for funding basic incomes for everyone. First, the solar systems pay for themselves, so they don't need continuous funding from taxes. As the solar dividend programs grew and reached more people, they did not add a continuously growing demand for more tax money.

Second, solar PV is modular, so adding a new increment of solar panels can cover each new person. There's no need to risk millions of dollars on huge power plants when a small loan can cover one individual's needs. That simple pattern repeats until the program includes everyone.

Third, solar electricity is a reliable source of income. While some months get more sun than others, the long-term average of solar energy arriving in a given location is dependable. The solar farms calculate the monthly solar dividends from that long-term average, not month-to-month production. And electricity is a commodity that will always be in demand.

And fourth, solar energy is available worldwide. This allowed every nation to set up solar systems within its borders to offer economic security for its own citizens. Locations with less sun required systems larger than ten kilowatts per person, but never more than twice as large. A few places with abundant wind power and little sun instead opted to build wind farms to generate solar dividends (since wind is powered by solar energy too).[1]

Initially, some poor countries with low rates of electricity consumption exported their excess solar electricity to countries with a higher demand, where they could afford to pay the higher price. The resulting inflow of solar dollars helped boost the poor countries out of poverty.

Their national economies remain stable because their energy source is local and secure. The great disparities that existed between rich and poor countries in the early 21st century are much reduced because the local solar energy source supports vital local economies.

The distributed nature of solar energy enabled remote rural areas not connected to the electrical grid to finally have energy services. Village power systems pumped water and refrigerated foods, boosted school attendance by freeing children from labor, and enabled a variety of entrepreneurial activities.

The world advanced toward economic fairness through energy. The goal was not economic equality, as people were still unequal based on their abilities and efforts. But solar dividends proved to be a fair way to distribute a basic share of nature's bounty to everyone.

Part A: A Vision of the Future

CHAPTER 4

Our Solar-Powered Economy in 2099

THE POPULARITY OF THE solar dividend program sped up the growth of solar electricity, which drove the decline of fossil fuels during the 21st century. Despite warnings to the contrary, the world's economy runs just fine on 100% solar energy.[1] It was not an overnight revolution, but a decades-long transition from fossil fuels to solar electricity.

Solar energy represents Earth's energy income, while fossil fuels represent Earth's energy savings account. The planet built up that savings account over millions of years from green plants that captured sunlight and stored it in the ground as coal, oil, and gas. The human race burned through that savings account for 200 years, drawing down that one-time gift of nature. Finally, in the 21st century, we transitioned from our dwindling savings account to our steady income.

While underway, each step of the transition felt permanent. Since solar energy is income, it will never be depleted. We won't need to switch energy sources again as long as we maintain the solar equipment. Now in 2099, solar energy supplies nearly 100% of energy services either directly or indirectly.

The direct solar supply comes primarily from ubiquitous photovoltaic panels. Today the nations of the world have installed a total of 100 terawatts (100 trillion watts) of solar PV panels. Although they're everywhere, hardly anyone notices them. They don't move or make noise, and they don't take up much space. A few technological innovations resolved the space issue early on.

When the solar dividend program was expanding rapidly, social conflicts arose over where to put the panels. Rooftops were the obvious choice, and many homeowners and businesses made money leasing their roofs to solar co-ops. Solar manufacturers integrated low-priced photovoltaic elements into roof shingles, tiles, and metal roof panels, so that most new or replacement roofs are photoactive and generate power even though they look like normal roofs.

For larger arrays, co-ops looked to build solar farms in the surrounding countryside. That put solar in conflict with agriculture. A solar farm can usually generate more money than can traditional farm crops. Farmers found they could sell their land for solar and retire early.

But in a world where population growth still strains the food supply, taking farmland out of food production to make energy was considered bad policy, if not immoral. Proposed solar farms met resistance from rural populations, and many local governments banned them to preserve their agricultural communities. In 2019 Oregon became the first US state to establish state-wide rules restricting solar development on prime agricultural land.[2]

So the co-ops took a lesson from their rooftop programs. When PV panels cover a roof, they don't take over the land and prevent people from living there. The property remains a living space *and* generates solar electricity. On farmland, the practice of *agrivoltaics* developed to merge farming with solar electricity. "In an agrivoltaic system, the environment under the panels is much cooler in the summer and stays warmer in the winters. This not only lessens rates of evaporation of irrigation waters in the summer, but it also means that plants don't get as stressed out" said agrivoltaics pioneer Greg Baron-Gafford.[3]

For crops that need full sun, a technological advance enabled such dual usage. As described earlier, installers can mount semitransparent PV panels—originally developed to cover greenhouses—over farmland. That maintains the agricultural use of the land, and the only change for the farmer is to work around the posts holding up the overhead racks—a bother, but the lease payments make it worthwhile. In some locations, pole-mounted PV installed along the boundaries between fields eliminated even that bother.

Today most PV installations are dual use, retaining the original function of the land, whether in an urban or rural setting. PV panels need not consume the land; they need access to the sky above the land. That works wherever the original use of the land can continue beneath solar panels.

The dual-use approach also resolved most of the conflicts over the ecological impacts of solar farms. Some early utility-scale solar farms in the California desert single-mindedly focused on maximizing output without regard to the environment. News stories about a project destroying desert tortoise habitat gave solar a bad name. Governments enacted land-use regulations to ensure solar farms integrated into their setting rather than overwhelming it, to keep their good environmental credentials.

Installing solar farms on degraded land often improved the land. Degraded lands resulting from clear cutting, dumping, chemical contamination, over grazing, mining, and agricultural depletion were the cheapest to lease for solar farms. The solar farms improved the ecosystem by controlling erosion, providing habitat for plant and animal species, and encouraging genetic diversity and pollinators.[4]

Sometimes solar farms aren't on land at all. Floating offshore platforms now support solar PV panels instead of oil drilling rigs.[5] Because PV arrays have a low profile compared to tall wind turbines, anchoring these so-called *floatovoltaic* arrays closer to shore doesn't draw complaints about the view.

Dam operators also floated rafts of panels on their reservoirs. Combining solar power during the day with hydropower during the night enabled the system to work as a reliable baseload electricity provider.[6] And the California State Water Project covered most of the hundreds of miles of their water transport canals with floatovoltaics, where they significantly reduce evaporation losses. The water beneath the panels also keeps them cool, improving their efficiency.[7]

Three forms of indirect solar energy supplement the energy supply: wind; hydropower; and waves. Together they can produce another 30 terawatts of electric power worldwide.

Most wind turbines in 2099 float far offshore. That situation developed from the basic economics of wind turbines. Doubling the blade length quadruples the energy output of a wind turbine, which encouraged designers to develop longer blades and taller towers to accommodate them. However, such tall structures generate complaints about visual pollution from miles away.

Wind-farm developers precluded such complaints by moving them far from shore, on floating structures anchored with cables to the seabed. That helped place them out of shipping lanes and in zones of unfettered wind.

Some floating wind and PV farms transmit power to the shore through underwater power cables. Where the distance is too great for cables, a farm will instead consume the electricity on the platform to split water and generate methanol, a liquid fuel that tanker ships can transport to shore. Onshore facilities use fuel cells to convert the methanol back to electricity.[8]

Methanol fuel cells also largely solved the general problem of energy storage and transport. Critics often faulted solar and wind for their intermittency. The sun doesn't always shine and the wind doesn't always blow when energy demand runs high. Utility companies brought online many energy storage systems based on batteries, pumped water, and flywheels, but the one solution that could scale to a 130-terawatt solar economy was methanol.

Making methanol by electrochemically combining carbon dioxide from the air with hydrogen pulled from water was an old but inefficient industrial process. New inexpensive catalysts improved the efficiency and allowed it to take off.[9] Now solar and wind farms can convert their excess electricity to liquid methanol, which they store in unpressurized steel tanks. When electricity demand exceeds supply, they pass the methanol to fuel cells to generate power. If they need more storage capacity, they just build bigger tanks. Methanol storage even made seasonal energy storage possible, letting them store excess energy captured during the summer to generate electricity during the winter.

Methanol fuel cells also eliminated the two major drawbacks of electric cars: long charging times and limited range. Instead of charging a car's batteries for hours from the grid, a car can quickly fill up on methanol fuel. Instead of burning the fuel, the onboard fuel cells recharge its batteries. When methanol fueling stations became commonplace, the limitations on the range of electric cars disappeared. Even long-haul trucks switched to electric motors and run on solar-generated methanol instead of diesel fuel.

Other modes of transportation also adapted to solar electricity. After the Great Energy Crisis made jet travel too expensive for most people, rail travel made a comeback, using electricity to power the trains. High-speed surface trains and even higher-speed evacuated tube trains could transport people nearly as fast as the old jetliners, without the carbon emissions of jet fuel.[10]

These transitions followed the general pattern of electrification of the economy. Because solar and wind generate electricity, not fuels, they could best be used by replacing fuel-burning devices with their electric equivalents.

Most engines that burn fossil fuels have disappeared, replaced by more efficient electric motors. Governments didn't ban engine fuel, but as it grew more expensive and harder to find, its use declined. The public treats fuel-engine operators like cigarette smokers: tolerated but frowned upon because of the noise, pollution, and carbon dioxide they produce.

Ship transportation steadily switched to solar energy. Most transport ships have a canopy of solar panels to power their electric motors. Many ships raise giant computer-controlled sails for wind propulsion. They make the sails from flexible PV material to generate extra electric power when the sun shines.[11] Ships also carry a tank of solar-generated methanol in reserve to use when neither sun nor wind is available.

Homes and commercial buildings gradually converted to 100% electric. Electric heat pumps replaced gas-fired space and water heaters, and cooking became fully electric. Over time, people replaced gas-fired yard tools with battery-powered models.

With few exceptions, even industrial operations transitioned to solar electricity. The steel industry had long used electric arc furnaces to make high-quality steel, so that industry's conversion from coal to electricity was straightforward.

Aluminum manufacturing already used electricity for most of its energy. The cement industry had to develop a new low-energy electrochemical technique for producing cement from electricity and concentrated solar heat instead of fossil fuels.[12]

Some industrial conversions were easy. The gigantic trucks used in mining operations already used electric motors on each wheel. They only had to replace the onboard diesel-powered generators with methanol fuel cells to power the wheel motors. In 2020 the Zaldívar Mine in northern Chile became the first 100% renewable-powered copper mine.[13]

Other industries still needing heat for processing materials continue to burn fuels. In some cases, they have converted to solar-generated methane, which replaces natural gas. In other cases, they continue to use natural gas but pay a surcharge to cover the cost of removing the equivalent amount of carbon from the atmosphere, making them carbon neutral.

Industrial food production underwent a complete transformation over the last century. Farming largely abandoned the old practice of plowing up the land and spreading fertilizer every year because of the high cost of fossil fuels. Farmers still grow food on the land, but they use permaculture that produces steady-state harvests without plowing.

Vertical food-production towers located in or around cities now grow much of our food using *aquaponics*. The plants grow in soil-free mediums fed with nutrients recycled from fish farms.[14] The light for photosynthesis comes from solar-powered grow lamps. Because food grows close to consumers, the food is fresher and requires less energy for processing, transportation, and refrigeration.

The other major energy industry that underwent a gradual transformation was the electric utility industry. Utility companies are no longer the primary generators of electricity. In the old days, utility companies generated most of the electricity they sold in their grid from fossil fuels and uranium. Now solar and wind systems owned by many people have largely supplanted those energy sources.

The old utility model of buying cheap raw energy, converting it to electricity, and selling that to their customers no longer applies. Utility companies now make their money by transporting and storing electricity. They still manage the grid of distribution wires and now charge a fee to transport electricity from where generated to where used. They also provide energy storage services, which allow those who generate solar electricity to shift the delivery to a time of day when the rates are higher by paying a small storage fee. With high electricity rates, utility companies still make enough profits.

CHAPTER 5

Carbon Emissions Under Control in 2099

IT SOUNDS HARD TO believe now, but early in the 21st century the world seemed reluctant to give up fossil fuels. Politicians believed that, because the economy was running on fossil fuels, they must keep supporting them or the economy would crash. Their belief might have been understandable if no suitable replacements for fossil fuels were available, but there were. Solar and wind already were supplying electricity with no carbon dioxide emissions, but the uptake of those new energy sources was too slow. The threat of global warming alone was not enough to accelerate the transition.

In the end, it was not the hazards of global warming that motivated the transition; rather, the popularity of solar dividends created a huge demand for solar power. Although saving the planet was insufficient reason to act, saving your family was.

The big downturn in carbon emissions that took place over the 21st century was driven more by solar dividends than by climate fears. Solar dividends stimulated the massive switch-over to solar electricity that finally allowed the world to wean itself from fossil fuels. As transportation, industry, and other parts of the world economy adapted to using abundant solar electricity, the demand for fossil fuels tilted down over the course of the century—and so did the resulting carbon emissions.

So much solar-based electricity became available that carbon extraction became possible. Pulling carbon dioxide out of the atmosphere requires energy, but burning fossil fuels for that purpose just added *more* carbon dioxide. Only carbon-free solar electricity could power the machines to pull carbon dioxide from the air and convert it to concrete.[1]

In the early 2070s the world's carbon emissions went net negative for the first time in modern history. That milestone signaled the success of the solar dividend program in achieving its second goal: to reduce global warming. It will take at least another century to rebalance our atmosphere and oceans back to preindustrial levels, but carbon dioxide levels are finally going in the right direction—downward.

The developers of solar dividends wisely promoted the program primarily as a basic income generator, with environmental gains as secondary benefits. Given the poor record of nations taking action on global warming, they wouldn't have supported the program if that was the only goal.

The more immediate problems of crushing poverty and economic insecurity that were stirring unrest proved to be better reasons for adopting solar energy, especially since solar paid for itself.

Once the solar dividend program proved successful, everyone wanted to get their share. Governments had to manage the process to set utility rates and make sure it was fair. The program grew on its own, and solar installations expanded at a record pace around the world.

The world had installed large amounts of solar and wind power by 2025, so that when the Great Energy Crisis hit and the price of fossil fuels skyrocketed, most of the world's economies survived. The crisis was triggered by the financial collapse of half of the world's major oil companies because they were overextended on debt pursuing expensive-to-extract unconventional oil and gas. The failures caused shortages that drove up prices.

Although the crisis created plenty of hardship, it accomplished three positive changes:

- The crisis raised energy prices, which made it easier to pay solar dividends.
- It revealed how unreliable fossil fuels were.
- It pushed nations to speed up their transition away from fossil fuels.

Solar dividends received a boost in 2032 when the United Nations responded to the hardships of the crisis by adding a new clause to the Universal Declaration of Human Rights—the right to a share of solar energy to support the life of every person.

We can credit solar dividends with the changeover from pessimism in the early 21st century to optimism as we enter the 22nd century. Solar dividends now provide basic economic security for nearly everyone in the world. And solar electricity powers our economy cleanly and sustainably. Those outcomes would have been unlikely without solar dividends.

We still need to pull out one crucial thread from this beautiful tapestry and examine it in more detail. That thread describes the transition in the *price* we paid for energy during the 21st century.

Part A: A Vision of the Future

CHAPTER 6

Energy Prices Went Up

THE THREE FAR-REACHING GLOBAL benefits of solar dividends didn't come for free. Utility regulators allowed electricity bills to rise incrementally to pay for solar dividends. The rates rose slowly, and the utility companies broadcast the changes ahead of time so people could adjust.

In the beginning, when pilot programs were first testing the solar dividends idea, the early data indicated that the program would fail. The principal problem was that utility companies were paying meager prices for any solar electricity that people fed into the power grid. Those feed-in rates were only two to five cents per kilowatt-hour. A typical ten-kilowatt solar array in a sunny location can generate about 13,000 kilowatt-hours per year, which at those prices meant a return of only $22 to $54 per month. Such small amounts wouldn't serve as a useful minimum basic income in most of the world.

One early trial in setting higher feed-in rates showed what positive effects they could achieve. Starting in 2000, Germany experimented with what they called *feed-in tariffs*. A feed-in tariff is a government policy that sets high feed-in rates that stimulate the growth of the solar industry and decline over time as the industry grows. Utilities initially paid PV owners a feed-in tariff as high as 43 Euro-cents (equivalent to U.S. $.57) per kilowatt-hour in 2004, reduced to 29 Euro-cents in 2011, and 17 Euro-cents in 2014.[1]

The experiment proved wildly successful. When businesses and homeowners learned they could make money by installing PV arrays, they jumped at the opportunity. They transformed Germany into the world's leading installer of PV hardware. The program grew so fast that the government finally had to scale it back because their utility grid was not prepared to handle such large amounts of variable input.

The German experiment contributed three lessons to the solar dividend program:

- Setting a high feed-in rate sufficed to stimulate mass installations of solar energy systems.
- The cost to government was small because the higher rates appeared on the utility bills that everyone paid.
- The opposition came from people without solar being forced to pay higher utility bills, complaining they saw no benefits for themselves.

A similar experiment in Japan achieved similar results. Energy regulators worldwide then applied these lessons when they developed what became the solar dividend programs we have today.

Here's how the solar feed-in rates work in 2099. Governments regulate feed-in rates today because they consider the electric grid an essential backbone of civilization and commerce. Solar arrays that are specifically set up and certified to provide solar dividends receive the highest feed-in rate. A solar co-op paying solar dividends to its members and subject to government inspection gets $1 per kilowatt-hour from the utility company.

From that $1, the co-op must pay out a solar dividend and cover any expenses. The expenses include:

- Leasing land, or more precisely, leasing the sky space above the land.
- A *wheeling fee*, which is the cost to transport the electricity to the consumer. That fee covers the costs for the utility to maintain its power lines and is proportional to the distance the energy travels. Most co-ops try to keep that fee low by delivering energy to local customers where possible.
- An energy storage fee, which the utility charges if it has to absorb excess solar electricity when demand is lower than supply. Some co-ops avoid that fee by establishing their own on-site energy storage facilities, so they can coordinate delivery to the utility based on demand.
- The co-op's operating expenses. These expenses are low because solar farms need little maintenance, and because co-ops automate the billing and payment operations.

A typical breakdown of expenses sees two cents per kilowatt-hour going for land lease, three cents going to the utility company for wheeling and storage charges, and two cents to cover the co-op's operating expenses. That leaves $.93 per kilowatt hour as the solar dividend paid to the member. If the member's ten-kilowatt solar system generates 13,000 kilowatt-hours per year, that amounts to about $12,000 per year, or about $1,000 per month in basic income.

A co-op's operating budget derived from its 2 percent share scales with the number of members it has. For example, a co-op operating solar farms for 10,000 members each with a ten-kilowatt solar section has an annual budget of about $2.6 million.

The utility company covers its expenses and makes its profits from the wheeling and storage fees. Although the rates may seem small, utility companies handle billions of kilowatt-hours per year from co-ops.

Utilities also carry billions of kilowatt-hours from solar and wind installations that aren't part of the solar dividend program. Since those systems aren't paying out solar dividends, they receive a lower feed-in rate per kilowatt-hour. These include homes and businesses with their own rooftop solar arrays and solar farms generating profits for shareholders. Those array owners pay the utility the same fees as co-ops for wheeling and storage.

The rate that consumers see on their utility bill is the weighted average of these two tiers, or about $.60 per kilowatt-hour in most places. This is considerably higher than the average electricity rate paid when the program began. In 2015, the average cost of electricity in the U.S. was about $.12 per kilowatt-hour, about one fifth of the current rate.

But utility customers in the U.S. and other countries weren't hit with a sudden jump in their bill. In the early years cheap fossil fuels still generated most electricity while utilities gradually folded in more of the expensive solar kilowatt-hours. Because the consumer's bill was the weighted average, they hardly noticed the effects of the first solar systems.

As more solar electricity came online, the solar payments increased and the average bill crept up (except for the bigger bump during the Great Energy Crisis when all energy prices rose). It took several decades for solar to replace all fossil fuels, so it took several decades for utility bills to reach their current levels.

The Solar Profit Margin

The utility rate structure of 2099 differs markedly from that at the start of the century. Back then the consumer price of energy hovered just above what it cost to produce the energy. If the cost to produce electricity went down, then competition would force the consumer price of electricity to go down as well.

The new rate structures mandated by governments now separate the production cost from the price consumers pay. Instead of pricing energy based on its production cost, regulators price it according to its value to society. As detailed in chapter 11, *The True Value of Solar Energy*, solar electricity delivers a high value, so it's assigned a high price.

The differential between its production cost and selling price defined the *solar profit margin*. The solar profit margin became the economic magic that made solar dividends successful. Governments justified requiring higher rates as the means for addressing the three otherwise intractable problems. The big jump in fossil fuel prices resulting from the Great Energy Crisis further justified the rise in prices for solar electricity.

Without the solar profit margin, payments for solar electricity would have been too low to help people out of poverty and too low to spur solar development. Without the solar profit margin, we would likely have succumbed to one, two, or all three of the global crises facing human civilization in the first two decades of the 21st century.

Part A: A Vision of the Future

CHAPTER 7

We Adapted to Higher Energy Prices

FEARS OF ECONOMIC DISASTER caused by intentionally raising energy prices turned out to be overblown. Those fears arose from memories of the oil shocks experienced in the 20th century, when world events triggered sudden spikes in oil prices, plunging national economies dependent on oil into turmoil.

This transition in the 21st century to higher energy prices proceeded on a more orderly path. Prices rose gradually according to a schedule, allowing people and businesses time to adapt. The primary mode of adapting was to use energy more efficiently.

A long period of cheap energy had shaped the energy-using systems in place at the start of the transition. The cheap prices resulted from oil companies exploiting fields of oil and gas as fast as possible to maximize profit. With energy so cheap, engineers gave little consideration to how efficiently it was used. Energy expenses registered as a negligible line item in the budget of most homes and businesses. Energy cost so little that even when you saved it, your bill didn't go down very much. People felt little incentive to save energy.

That wasteful design approach changed when energy prices went up, because suddenly, saving energy paid off. Most consumers found they had plenty of room for improvement because their existing energy hardware was so inefficient. Swapping out such equipment for models that used less energy paid back more quickly with higher energy prices.

Also, energy-using habits changed once the higher energy prices surfaced in people's minds. Energy-wasting practices could no longer be ignored once energy was no longer dirt-cheap.

Many people adapted to the higher prices by installing their own solar energy systems. Homes and businesses with properly exposed roof spaces could generate their own electricity with PV panels. Every kilowatt-hour they produced and consumed reduced their utility bill by $.60, the retail cost of the electricity they would have had to buy. At that rate the payback period for installing the solar was just a few years.

Those individuals without access to the sun were stuck paying the higher rates, but they had redress—they could sign up for the solar dividend program. The added income more than covered their higher electricity bills.

New adult participants had two choices at sign-up: they could pay directly for their solar installation at the co-op and start receiving monthly dividends immediately, or they could forego paying up front and give the solar system time to pay for itself, deferring dividends for several years.

Solar dividends created their own snowball effect, whereby rising energy prices that paid for solar dividends motivated more people to join. That helped speed up the effort to reach everyone.

It might appear that these are circular payments, wherein you pay higher utility bills so you can receive solar dividends back. Where is the net benefit?

First, individuals don't use all the electricity their ten-kilowatt solar system generates. Per capita residential energy use in the US averages 4,400 kilowatt-hours per year. That's only about a third of the 13,000 kilowatt-hours that their solar system generates. So the solar system raises three times the money that the customer has to pay.

Second, many utility regulators retained Lifeline rates, where the first quota of electricity is charged at a low rate to help low-income people. Only if your electricity use goes above the Lifeline quota are you charged at the higher rates. Wealthy people generally use more electricity and therefore pay a higher share of the premium rates.

Third, only individuals can receive solar dividends to help them pay for their higher utility bills. Commercial businesses, industry, governments, and organizations aren't eligible. Those entities consume about two thirds of all electricity, and their payments largely fund solar dividends for individuals.

Those institutional consumers responded to the higher utility rates in two ways. They started using energy more efficiently to lower their energy expenses, and they passed on the remaining increased energy costs by charging more for their products or services.

Passing on the added energy costs had the general effect of driving up prices of everything. But the effect on the economy was not as large as the energy price increases because energy was only one component of many that made up a product's price.[1]

As complaints came in about rising prices for goods and services, some businesses discovered how much energy they wasted and could therefore save in order to gain a competitive advantage. When energy prices double, if you use half as much energy then your utility bill won't go up at all.

Individuals responded similarly. Although solar dividends helped people pay their higher bills, it didn't take long for people to realize they could keep more of their monthly solar dividend if they became more efficient in their energy use.

Because governments were partially responsible for the higher utility bills by mandating high solar feed-in rates, they instituted programs to help people and businesses become more energy efficient. It helped that these were planned price rises, based on the expected rate of rollout of solar dividends. That predictability removed economic uncertainty and provided a solid basis for estimating return on investment from energy efficiency measures, even those planned for the future.

The higher energy prices produced another effect: Throwaway goods became a thing of the past. Throwaway goods were possible only because of cheap energy. Once the energy that went into making and transporting goods became more expensive, the price of throwaway goods went way up.

As a result, expensive energy created an incentive for making goods more durable. Spending shifted from throwaways, which were no longer cheap, to durable goods, which were also not cheap but lasted much longer.

This led to other knock-on effects: reduced landfill trash, reduced plastic waste in the oceans, and reduced demand for mining raw materials.

These changes helped solve a problem that economists were already worried about: many raw resources were becoming too depleted to continue the practice of once-through processing from mining to landfill in the so-called "linear economy". The deepening scarcity of resources finally made it cheaper to recycle than to mine afresh, shifting us into a more "circular economy" better suited to ecological and economic sustainability.[2]

For example, Finland's state-of-the-art rubbish dump, the Ämmässuo Waste Treatment Centre in Espoo outside Helsinki, recycles 100% of what goes into it. They require source separation, offering lower customer rates for better separation. The plant sends out glass, paper, plastics, and cartons for remanufacturing. They ferment organic materials into methane, and any leftover organic waste becomes compost.[3]

Many countries adopted "cradle-to-cradle" laws.[4] Such laws require every product to have a plan for shepherding it from cradle to cradle, a step beyond cradle to grave, wherein the grave would be the landfill. That meant manufacturers had to design products for complete recycling at the end of their useful life, so their materials and components could go back into new products. Such laws encouraged the design of longer-lasting products to reduce the frequency of recycling.

Part A: A Vision of the Future

CHAPTER 8

Massive Boost to the Economy

THE ONGOING SOLAR DIVIDEND program generates a triple boost to the economy.

- It built a huge solar energy industry that employs vast armies of people to make panels and install solar farms worldwide.
- It puts ready cash in everyone's pocket to spend on goods and services, which increases overall economic activity and creates additional non-solar jobs.
- It recycles energy payments into the local community instead of exporting them out to remote fossil fuel producers, stopping a significant drain on local economies. Money kept in local circulation is typically spent several times, creating a multiplier effect for jobs and businesses.

Solar farms and other solar and wind installations enhance every local economy that builds them. They contribute a stable and reliable source of energy that is not subject to world events or economic downturns.

In a real sense, solar acts like a local oil well for generating wealth. Solar panels take something for free from nature (sunshine) and convert it to something with real economic value (electricity). That process occurs everywhere, not just in the few locations where drillers find oil underground. Every local economy creates primary wealth from its sunshine.

Every region extends that new energy wealth by using it more efficiently. In response to higher electricity prices, energy efficiency businesses blossomed. Spending on efficiency improvements created a whole new class of jobs that could not be offshored.

Once the results from the first pilot programs for solar dividends came in, politicians quickly got on board. They judged that the economic benefits of the program far exceeded the costs, and they could see it would be popular because it helped everyone.

Politicians could promise the equivalent of "a chicken in every pot" without having to pay for it, because the solar energy systems paid for themselves. All they had to do was adjust the feed-in rates that utilities pay for solar electricity.

The solar dividend program appealed to both conservatives and liberals because it provided many different reasons to support it.

Seven Reasons Liberals Support Solar Dividends:

1. It includes all people, eventually.
2. It helps raise up the poor.
3. It shares a worldwide natural resource among all people.
4. It helps people be more economically self-reliant.
5. It enhances a sense of community.
6. It gives everyone the dignity of self-support without the stigma of welfare.
7. It's not susceptible to being taken over by the rich.

Seven Reasons Conservatives Support Solar Dividends:

1. It doesn't require an increase in income taxes.
2. Because the money is not collected and distributed by the government, it doesn't create a large government bureaucracy but instead uses existing regulatory agencies.
3. It avoids monthly government examination of your income to determine eligibility.
4. It helps people be more economically self-reliant.
5. It supports entrepreneurs trying to get started.
6. It supports individual freedom of choice on how to take part in a market economy.
7. It reduces economic migration by generating income for everyone where they live.

Even those who didn't believe the science of climate change found they could support solar energy, not because it fixes global warming, but because it provides economic benefits to ordinary people, including themselves.

Once politicians on both sides became advocates, things happened quickly. Governments enabled solar dividends by setting high feed-in rates to pay for them. They established the rules and regulations for solar co-ops to ensure they operated in the interests of their members. In some jurisdictions they even assisted solar co-ops by locating solar farms on government buildings, parking lots, and closed municipal landfills.

Although many people and businesses grumbled about paying higher utility bills, a consensus emerged that this approach was better than paying higher income taxes to solve the stubborn problems of economic insecurity, energy supply, and climate change. Paying a higher utility bill seemed like a relatively easy way to save the world.

Part A: A Vision of the Future

Building That Future

Introduction to Part B

The future described in Part A could be your story or your child's or grandchild's story. But that future won't materialize by itself. Our current world continues to hold to a trajectory aimed at disaster brought on by the combined menaces of rising inequality, global warming, and unsustainable energy. All three threats continue to grow, showing that whatever efforts have so far been made to address them aren't working.

Albert Einstein once wrote, "a new type of thinking is essential if mankind is to survive and move toward higher levels." He was speaking of the risk of nuclear war, but his words resonate today because we face our own triad of threats to our existence. It's time for some new thinking.

Here's my contribution—establish a program to set up PV panels to generate solar dividends for everyone in the world.

Since this has never been done, we have to invent how to proceed. Here in Part B we return to the present and I describe how we can build this program from scratch. I'll provide more detail about how high solar feed-in rates enable co-ops to manage solar farms and deliver solar dividends. But since setting high feed-in rates may be politically and economically controversial, I also present alternative approaches.

This idea is huge, and I don't claim to have all the answers. As we sort out the issues this idea raises, remember that it is based on a simple fact: no one owns the sun. The value that the sun delivers to our planet every day in the form of solar energy is part of our commons, something that can and should be shared among all people.

This part discusses how we can deliver that economic value to everyone on Earth as solar dividends.

CHAPTER 9

Unconditional Basic Income

My solution builds on an idea others have proposed, an *unconditional basic income*. That's a program whereby society grants everyone a small income, with the goals of reducing poverty and enhancing personal freedom. In such a program, society makes regular unconditional payments to every person without regard to work status, other income, or family arrangement. The amounts can vary depending on the plan; they range from a small supplement up to enough to live on without working. The purpose is to lift every individual out of grinding poverty onto an economic platform from which they can build their life.

Versions of this concept are now showing up in news reports because governments and social institutions recognize that many traditional jobs are gone and aren't coming back. The idea goes by various names, including Universal Basic Income, Basic Income Guarantee, Minimum Income, Citizen's Income,

Guaranteed Annual Income, and Unconditional Basic Income (UBI), the name I use in this book.

These characteristics define a UBI:[1]

- **Periodic:** payments arrive at regular intervals (for example every month), not as a one-off grant.
- **Cash payment:** payments are in cash, allowing those who receive it to decide how they spend it. It is not paid in kind (such as food or services) or in vouchers dedicated to a specific use.
- **Individual:** payments go to individuals—and not, for instance, to households.
- **Unconditional:** payments aren't contingent on working or showing a willingness to work.
- **Universal:** payments go to everyone, not excluding the well-off.

Some wonder: Why include the well-off if they don't need the money? That feature keeps the program simple, because determining eligibility requires an expensive and intrusive bureaucracy to track incomes. The other reason is fairness. If everyone receives the same amount of money, no constituency will oppose it because no one gets left out.

Interestingly, the rich are the ones who benefit the least from a basic income. To them, the basic income payments amount to spare change. Those who will benefit the most are those with the least. The poorer you are the more you gain in proportion to any other income. To a single mother with children and a low-paying job, it could make a big difference. To a poor farmer in India, it could transform his life. An unconditional basic income achieves fairness by being egalitarian, while the effects and perceived benefits of the money are felt most by the poor. It's self-adjusting that way.

Some economists express concern that a free basic income would remove the incentive to work. Taken to the extreme, if everyone were living off a basic income and no one worked, society would slow to a halt. However, the limited research to date on basic incomes doesn't show this effect. Researcher Ioana Marinescu says "The evidence does not suggest an average worker will drop out of the labor force when provided with unconditional cash, even when the transfer is large."[2] Payments are only big enough to survive on, not enough to be too comfortable. Most people would choose to work to improve their life beyond basic survival. Many would rather work if the occupation stimulates and challenges.

Another concern is that payments to children might become an incentive for families to have more children just to increase their income. In the program described in this book, the money for children doesn't go to the parents but to an escrow account held until the child reaches maturity.

The idea of basic incomes isn't new. Thomas Paine, author of *Common Sense*, proposed a basic income as far back as 1796 in a pamphlet titled *Agrarian Justice*. Many prominent economists, including John Stuart Mill, John Kenneth Galbraith, Friedrich Hayek, and Milton Friedman have advocated for a basic income of some form.

For example, Milton Friedman proposed a type of minimum income in the form of a *negative income tax*. In that plan, if a person's income as reported on their federal income tax form showed they were below a certain minimum, the government refunded money to reach that minimum. President Richard Nixon proposed it in 1971 as part of a welfare reform package, but Congress never approved it.

No country has ever implemented an unconditional basic income program for all its citizens, so why would anyone propose this now?

One reason is to reduce the growing gap between the rich and poor, which is reaching unsustainable levels. Oxfam reports that the richest 1% of humanity owns as much wealth as the remaining 99%.[3] In addition:

> Today, some 4.3 billion people—more than 60 percent of the world's population—live in debilitating poverty, struggling to survive on less than the equivalent of $5 per day. Half do not have access to enough food. And these numbers have been growing steadily over the past few decades.
>
> —Jason Hickel[4]

Thomas Piketty's landmark book *Capital in the Twenty-First Century* uses current trends to project that the coming decades will be marked by an inevitable progression toward increased inequality of both income and wealth.[5]

Advocates say we should start providing basic incomes now because history has shown that a high level of inequality in a society portends the collapse of that society.[6] In a modern economy, growing inequality threatens its consumer base—not enough people will earn enough to buy the goods put up for sale. A basic income places money in the hands of people who will spend it and keep the economy moving.

We should start basic incomes now because the nature of work is changing. Computers, artificial intelligence, and robots are taking over jobs, making it more difficult for people willing to work to find employment capable of supporting them. A report from the McKinsey Global Institute says "60 percent of occupations have at least 30 percent of constituent work activities that could be automated".[7] Martin Ford, author of *Rise of the Robots: Technology and the Threat of a Jobless Future*, says a basic income guarantee best solves the problem of jobs becoming unavailable because of automation.[8]

In modern society, if you don't have your own business you need a job to live and support your family. Yet in many places there are more people than jobs. By requiring a job to survive, but not having enough jobs, we put people in impossible situations.

We should also start basic incomes now to help people who work hard in jobs that pay too little to support their families, or who toil in unreliable "gig" jobs such as Uber driving, or who must work nonpaying jobs like providing care for children or the elderly. Such workers constitute the "precariat" class, named for their precarious position in society.[9]

We should do this now to remove the unintended traps that keep people in welfare programs. One example is the US Social Security Disability Insurance program. "Once a person is approved for disability payments, any attempt to work beyond that point carries the danger of losing both the income and the accompanying health care benefits. As a result, virtually no one who gets into the program ever works again," says author Martin Ford.[10]

We should do this now because of political trends toward attaching work requirements to welfare when jobs are hard to find, forcing many people off of welfare and into poverty.

And we should do this now to give everyone an added measure of something most people value: freedom. Basic incomes help people balance work and family commitments more freely, allow more flexible forms of employment or self-employment, and provide an independent income for women to promote gender equality.

Today, a handful of countries are reviving the idea of basic incomes to respond to changing employment trends, although most programs fail the test of universality. Finland recently had an experimental basic income program to address two problems—fewer jobs available due to automation, and low wages for existing jobs. But to receive payments you must have been unemployed for at least a year or have less than six months of job experience.

Brazil's Bolsa Família program provides basic incomes for poor families, but it requires recipients to visit health clinics regularly and/or meet minimum school attendance requirements. While these are desirable goals, they require a bureaucracy to monitor and review such behaviors.

These conditions for inclusion show how conflicted politicians can be about approving basic incomes for everyone. Certainly "free money" would be popular with voters, but money is not free, so the funds for basic incomes must come from somewhere. In most basic income plans the money comes from taxes, and that's where most basic income plans run into trouble.

A UBI funded from income taxes creates a built-in conflict between taxed workers and UBI recipients. That conflict means political support for a UBI can easily shift, putting the program in jeopardy. A clear-cut example occurred in Ontario, Canada. The Ontario provincial government started a three-year pilot program for unconditional basic incomes in 2017. The election of 2018 put a more conservative government in place, and it immediately canceled the program despite suggesting they would keep it during the campaign.

In the United Kingdom, when pollsters described the concept of an unconditional basic income to people without telling them the funding source, 49% responded positively, while only 26% responded negatively. But if they were then informed that the basic income entailed an increase in income taxes, the support flipped, with only 30% supporting it and 40% opposing it.[11]

A similar survey in Finland found that while 70% of Finns supported the idea of basic incomes, that number drops to 35% when respondents learn that already high income taxes would have to increase to cover the cost of the program.[12]

These responses emerge from the basic human sense of fairness. The initial response shows that many people think our current economic system is unfair and that a basic income would help correct that. The subsequent response shows that people think it's unfair to take money from working people in the form of higher taxes to pay people who might not be working, so they oppose it.

> Forcing workers to pay for a UBI for those unwilling to work may be seen as inherently exploitive.
> —Institute for Policy Research[13]

Studies have shown that people don't object to economic inequality per se, but to economic unfairness. Some inequality is acceptable based on merit, but unfairness generates a strong dislike. "We should aspire to fair inequality, not unfair equality" says Mark Shekin of Yale University.[14]

Any proposal for unconditional basic incomes must address the issue of fairness. Most people recognize when a situation seems unfair. That you can't always explain *why* you experience a situation as unfair suggests that fairness registers more as a feeling than as a mental choice.

Research over several decades has shown that this sense of fairness derives from our genetic makeup. It has been observed throughout history and across cultures, in babies as young as fifteen months, and in animals such as chimpanzees, capuchin monkeys, and dogs. Fairness is a fundamental part of our being.

The survey responses described above show that any plan for changing the economy must be fair to receive broad public support. That's why UBI plans based on income taxes have had such a hard time gaining traction.

Nontrivial basic income programs demand a lot of money. A common phrase critiquing such programs is "an affordable basic income would be inadequate, and an adequate basic income would be unaffordable". Most economic studies have shown a basic income would need a large increase in taxes to fund it.[15] "In short, unless we are prepared to significantly increase taxes, a pure universal basic income is unaffordable" says Michael Tanner of the Cato Institute.

Yet despite such pessimistic assessments of the costs, the call for unconditional basic incomes continues to grow. The United Nations frames the issue in terms of human rights:

> The starting point is to acknowledge that economic insecurity represents a fundamental threat to human rights. It is not only a threat to the enjoyment of economic and social rights, even though they are a principal concern. Extreme inequality, rapidly increasing insecurity, and the domination of politics by economic elites in many countries, all threaten to undermine support for, and ultimately the viability of, the democratic systems of governance upon which the human rights framework depends.
>
> —UN Human Rights Council[16]

The social arguments in favor of basic incomes might be sound, but raising income taxes to pay for them doesn't pass the test of fairness for most people. But what if we could fund basic incomes from a different source?

CHAPTER 10

Solar Dividends as Basic Incomes

> The big issue with a universal basic income is not whether it is desirable but whether it is feasible.
>
> —Compass UK[1]

IF WE COULD PAY for basic incomes without raising income taxes, then we could pass the test of fairness and gain broad support. So instead of using income taxes for basic incomes, we should use solar energy.

Everyone knows solar energy improves the environment. Electricity produced from solar and wind doesn't pollute the air or water and doesn't emit greenhouse gases that contribute to global warming. For these reasons solar and wind are being deployed worldwide.

But solar energy has an even larger role to play because it can generate money. A solar panel exposed to the sun generates electricity that can be sold for cash.

The idea here is to hitch the horse of solar energy to pull the wagon of basic incomes. In a nutshell: society invests in solar energy equipment to generate electricity which it sells to the utility company. We distribute the cash to members of society as a dividend, forming the beginnings of an unconditional basic income not funded by income taxes.

By converting the inexhaustible supply of solar energy into electricity using PV panels, we can create an inexhaustible source of money. The amount of money varies with the size of PV array, the local sunshine conditions, and the local feed-in rate for electricity.

Appendix A, *Do The Numbers Add Up?* provides a formula for computing the annual amount. For a given location and size of an array, the feed-in rate becomes the crucial determinant of how big the generated income can be. In the future scenario described in Part A, the feed-in rate had risen to about $1.00 per kilowatt-hour, which produced a basic income of $1,000 per month.

A feed-in of $1.00 per kilowatt-hour is substantially higher than what most utility companies pay today for any solar electricity they receive and distribute. If instead the rate was similar to the $.57 that German utilities paid for solar electricity in 2004, then the basic income would be closer to $500 per month.[2] A feed-in rate of only $.10 per kilowatt-hour would generate less than $100 per month.

Although the amount will vary, the basic idea can work almost everywhere on the planet. If properly set up, that money could fund basic incomes for everyone. This kind of basic income can succeed where others fail because the funding does not come from income taxes.

We could call this merger of basic incomes and solar energy something like an "Unconditional Basic Income Paid For With

Money Derived From Solar Energy," but I suggest something shorter: *solar dividends*.

Like other basic income programs, solar dividends are paid directly at regular intervals in local money. They're paid to an individual, not to a household, and they aren't *means tested*, a process that determines eligibility based on current means of support from income, employment status, or family arrangement.

While meeting the definition of a basic income, solar dividends differ in several ways from other basic income proposals. The differences make their adoption more likely.

The biggest difference comes from the source of money to pay for them—not from income taxes, but from an investment in a revenue-generating solar energy array. This difference alone will overcome much of the resistance that other basic income plans encounter.

Reinventing a basic income as an investment means that once the panels pay off their installation costs, the dividends will flow indefinitely. No government need allocate part of its annual budget for it. Income taxes wouldn't need to be raised to support it.

In contrast, a tax-funded UBI imposes a permanent load on a government's budget. Once any unconditional basic income gets established and people come to rely on it, any attempts to cut back the program would disrupt people's lives and incite social conflict. If an economic downturn diminishes income tax revenues, then the government must scale back either basic incomes or other programs. Few politicians are willing to commit to such a trap. Solar dividends put no such burden on a government's budget.

Using investments to generate basic incomes is not a new idea. Most such proposals suggest creating a huge fund of money invested in stocks and bonds, whose annual dividends pay for basic incomes. That's how the Alaska Permanent Fund works. Starting in 1976, the state of Alaska deposited royalties from oil leases into a fund whose investment generates dividends. The fund distributes dividends equally to all Alaska residents.

Any government that doesn't own a big oil fund would have to assemble one from taxes. Unless the government has a tax surplus, it would have to divert money from other programs or raise taxes, neither of which would be popular. Also, the return on investment will vary year to year as it tracks the stock market. The annual Alaska dividends have fluctuated up and down, delivering $2,069 in 2008, $870 in 2012, and $1,600 in 2018. Notice that less is available in a downturn (2012), a time when many people would need more. Fluctuations in the stock market would not affect dividends generated by solar energy with regulated prices.

The second major difference of solar dividends is that the program need not be run by a government. Certainly the government would play a role in setting up the conditions and enforcing the rules, but the dividend money would not flow into and out of government coffers. Nongovernmental institutions like co-ops can work directly with utility companies to generate and pay solar dividends.

A government could run it, but would always be tempted to redirect the revenue generated from solar energy to other competing priorities. For example, in 2017 the Alaska oil dividend was estimated to be $2,300, but the Alaska legislature reduced it to $1,100 to balance their budget.

The third difference of solar dividends is that they won't be universal at the start. That is, the program can't grant dividends to everyone when the program begins, due to the physical impossibility of building enough solar arrays for everyone at once. That's why I've called them *unconditional* basic incomes rather than *universal* basic incomes.

Instead, the program will grow over time as co-ops organize and start building solar arrays. A lottery could distribute the first solar array sections to ensure fairness. Some programs may decide to grant the first systems to low-income people so the dividends do the greatest good. That will ensure greater impact in the early stages and get around the objection many people have about giving money to rich people. That change would require applicants to be means tested, but only once to get enrolled, not continuously as with other welfare programs. Gradually the program would expand to include everyone to satisfy the principle of sharing solar energy universally. It will probably take two generations before we can say that unconditional solar dividends become universal.

But the program doesn't have to reach everyone at once to have an impact. Those people lucky enough to win the initial selection lotteries would receive dividends that can change their lives. The impacts on society as a whole would be small at first, but would grow as the program covers more people.

Viewed from a world perspective, the solar dividend program can achieve a broad level of universality in the long run. The ultimate goal of solar dividends is universality on a global scale, a reach far greater than any national or state basic income program.

Universality is possible because sunshine bathes the planet without regard to national boundaries, type of government, or national wealth. You couldn't ask for a more egalitarian energy source. The bounty of this rich source of energy can and should be shared by everyone. We're all equal under the sun.

Some skeptics worry that giving people free money would make them lazy. That worry has its roots in taxpayer-funded welfare. It's a judgment that's almost universally applied to poor people.

As E. Y. Harburg put it in the libretto of the musical *Finian's Rainbow*:

> *When a rich man doesn't want to work, He's a bon vivant, yes, he's a bon vivant. But when a poor man doesn't want to work, He's a loafer, he's a lounger, He's a lazy good for nothing, he's a jerk.*

Many rich people don't work, but live off their investments. Do we call them lazy and take away their money to force them to work? No, we leave them alone because they're self-sufficient. With a basic income generated by solar energy, each person becomes self-sufficient too, even the poor.

If individuals can live off their solar dividends, there's no call to judge them as lazy. It's not a question of whether recipients of solar dividends deserve the money; they have a right to it. The co-op grants that right under the co-op's bylaws sanctioned by the state. As long as the recipient follows the rules of the co-op, the co-op cannot take away their solar dividends.

No one should think the poor are receiving payments for contributing nothing, because the payments are not for nothing: they are a royalty resulting from the participant's solar equipment generating valuable carbon-free electricity that helps power the economy. They supply a legitimate service, and we should respect the solar royalties as legitimate income.

By investing money in solar instead of giving away welfare money, we provide people the means to *make* money by producing valuable solar electricity. In the "makers versus takers" debate, solar dividends move everyone to the "maker" side.

In summary, solar dividends bring all the advantages of income tax-based unconditional basic incomes but overcome most of the disadvantages. The next chapter describes the details of how we make this program work.

CHAPTER 11

The True Value of Solar Energy

PART A OUTLINED a future in which co-ops set up everyone with an array of solar panels and distribute the benefits as solar dividends. That's an enormous project, but installing the panels is the easy part.

The difficult part comes from changing how society values energy. To have enough wealth to spread, the price of energy needs to rise so we can generate a sufficient solar profit margin. This is the crucial step that determines the success or failure of the program.

In chapter 6, *Energy Prices Went Up*, I described a future where electric companies have evolved from power generators to service providers. They take in power from myriad solar and wind generators spread over their territory and deliver the power to energy consumers, acting as an energy switchyard instead of an energy producer. They issue utility bills and collect payments according to rate tables set up by government regulatory bodies. They keep some money to pay for their energy transport and storage services, but otherwise pass through most of the customer payments to the creators of the power.

In my future scenario, if the power generator is a solar co-op set up to distribute solar dividends, then the co-op receives $1.00 per kilowatt-hour for the electricity it generates. That income to the co-op is higher than the expense of installing and maintaining the solar panels. The difference establishes a solar profit margin that allows the co-op to pay out the dividends that support its members.

The $1.00 per kilowatt-hour feed-in rate serves as a benchmark example in this book, a target to aim for. At that rate, a ten-kilowatt PV system that generates 13,000 kilowatt-hours per year could deliver a $12,000 annual basic income after expenses are subtracted. According to the PVWatts calculator available from the US National Renewable Energy Laboratory, a ten-kilowatt PV system in an average location generates that much. For example, such a system in Indianapolis in the US Midwest would generate 13,791 kilowatt-hours per year. Sunny Phoenix, Arizona would need only 8 kilowatts of PV to generate that much electricity, while a system in cloudy Seattle Washington would need 12 kilowatts of panels.[1]

Anyone familiar with electricity rates will immediately notice that a feed-in rate of $1 per kilowatt-hour is much higher than what utility companies in most locations are paying for solar electricity. It's even higher than the highest retail rates that people pay on their bill. Are such rates feasible?

Note that small roof-mounted systems on homes and businesses usually have a special *net metering* arrangement unrelated to feed-in rates. With net metering, the utility company credits the PV owner for any kilowatt-hours it feeds into the grid, and uses those credits to offset electricity the consumer draws from the grid. The grid acts as a virtual storage system for the PV owner. This is a good deal for the system owner, because they are essentially receiving the retail rate for their excess electricity. But at the end of the year, any kilowatt-hours over and above what the customer consumed earn only a trivial amount, if anything. So net metering is not useful beyond personal consumption.

The solar farms that generate solar dividends will not use net metering, but will negotiate feed-in rates with their utility company, under the supervision of utility regulators.

Governments already regulate utility company rates because they operate as natural monopolies. Most regions have a single electric company to avoid having multiple sets of competing power lines crowding utility poles. Since customers have no choice in their electricity provider, governments regulate such single providers to prevent price gouging of their captive customers.

Today utility companies typically pay large-scale independent solar electricity generators a feed-in rate of 5 to 10 cents per kilowatt-hour. Such feed-in rates paid to a solar co-op would generate only $50 to $100 per month, far short of a basic income.

The current low solar rates come from having to compete against conventional sources of electricity generated from fossil fuels. Utility regulators can set higher feed-in rates for solar if their state or country has established Renewable Energy Portfolio Standards.[2] Such standards specify a percentage of utility electricity that must come from renewable sources in order to meet climate goals, promote local energy production, and spur economic development.

But market price pressure combined with the declining cost of building solar arrays is driving down those feed-in rates. The high feed-in rates described in the Part A future scenario are unlikely to happen by market mechanisms alone. They will require a political decision by a government to enact rates above market rates.

On one side of the transaction, governments will have to regulate utilities to require such premium payments, and on the other, governments will regulate solar co-ops to avert fraud. Why would a government take those steps? By doing so, they can accomplish three major social goals: lift everyone out of poverty, reduce everyone's carbon footprint, and establish sustainable local sources of energy. These goals would be achieved not by budgeting line items and raising income taxes to fund them, but by raising utility rates for electricity users.

The surprising thing about this approach is that the effects on utility bills will not be noticed for many years. Keep in mind that the $1 per kilowatt-hour rate does not apply to all electricity sources, only to the electricity generated by solar co-ops for the purpose of solar dividends. Even with aggressive growth rates, it takes time to organize co-ops and build solar farms for large numbers of people.

While the first solar dividend farms are being built, there would be no increase in utility bills at all because no solar dividend electricity would be produced at the higher rate. When the first farms begin operating, then they collect $1.00 for each kilowatt-hour they generate, which will add to the utility company costs, and those costs will be passed through to their customers. At first, the solar dividend electricity is a tiny fraction of the total kilowatt-hours distributed by the utility company, so the effect on bills will be negligible. See the section titled "Why won't utility bills go up quickly?" in Appendix A for more details.

As more solar farms are built and more solar dividend kilowatt-hours are produced, bills will go up gradually in proportion to the growth in the solar output's fraction of total electricity. If in the future the solar dividends program manages to grow large enough to generate half the total electricity supply, then half of each utility bill would be charged at $1.00 per kilowatt-hour. If the other half were charged at 12 cents per kilowatt-hour, then the bill would average out to 56 cents per, not $1.00.[3]

How much bills actually go up depends on many other factors that go into utility rates. The nominal price per kilowatt-hour today is based on a utility's mix of energy sources, including fossil fuels like coal and natural gas; renewables like solar, wind, and hydropower; and nuclear power. Utilities then adjust that nominal price for many reasons. For example, utilities often charge more during peak usage times, less on weekends and holidays, more for those customers exceeding their basic quotas, and less for bulk rates to big industrial customers.

Utility rates also differ widely by region. The average residential utility rate in the U.S. is 12 cents per kilowatt-hour, but in Hawaii it ranges from 37 to 43 cents because that state imports a lot of fossil fuels to generate its electricity. Electricity consumers in Denmark pay 33 cents (US), while those in the Solomon Islands pay 88 to 99 cents.[4]

The biggest factor determining rates for residential users is how much electricity they use per month. Most utilities have set up tiered pricing, starting with Lifeline rates and going up as you use more. For example, California's Pacific Gas & Electric Company sets up three tiers for residential service. The bottom tier called the Baseline Usage rate in 2019 costs 22 cents per kilowatt-hour, the middle tier covering 101% to 400% of Baseline usage goes for 28 cents, and the top High Usage tier above 400% costs 49 cents per kilowatt-hour.[5] Compare that 49 cent rate that exists today to the 56 cent rate when solar dividends reach half the supply many years in the future. Solar dividend rates are higher, but not outlandish.

Under certain circumstances, people are willing to pay extremely high electricity rates, such as when they buy disposable batteries. Even if you buy a jumbo pack of AAA batteries, you'll pay at least $.50 per battery. The cost of the electricity in that battery amounts to an astounding $290 per kilowatt-hour, almost 300 times the proposed solar dividend rate.[6] The tiny amount of electricity and its portable form make such rates acceptable.

If the solar dividend program succeeds, then after several decades of growth a major part of all electricity will carry a premium price. Yet that higher price will deliver a long list of benefits.

The solar dividend program is based on an unconventional proposition: *charge more for energy* to gain greater benefits than you get with cheap energy. You can almost hear economists gasping in horror at such a suggestion. They will dismiss the idea out of hand because it defies the conventional wisdom that the economy functions best when energy is cheap.

That conventional wisdom keeps us locked into fossil fuels and inhibits us from aggressively responding to the climate crisis. It drains the courage from politicians negotiating climate treaties, making them afraid to upset the economic cart.

Such conventional wisdom derives from a history of economic growth that was enabled by the prevalence of cheap fossil fuels. Before fossil fuels, agriculture powered society by growing the food to fuel all human and animal labor. Since 90 percent of people were engaged in growing food, that left few free to make other things.

At the start of the Industrial Revolution, inventors created machines that automated making goods like textiles. One person running a machine could do the work of many performing the same task manually. But the machines required energy, and the main source of mechanical power at the time came from water wheels, long used for grinding grain.

Early textile factories competed for sites suitable for water wheels, and those sites quickly filled up. A shortage of water power inhibited the further expansion of mechanized manufacturing.

The nascent Industrial Revolution was rescued by the steam engine, first developed to pump water from mines, and later adapted to run factory machinery. The inefficient steam engines of the day consumed enormous amounts of fuel, and they rapidly depleted local wood supplies. Steam engines took off when coal replaced wood as the fuel. That change marked the start of the Fossil Fuel Age.

The free markets in coal, oil, and natural gas have long kept the price of fossil fuels low. Since we don't pay nature for the raw material of fossil fuels, the only costs come from extracting them from the ground, refining them, and transporting them. When an energy company sells fossil fuels on the market, it's competing with other producers primarily on price. Those that have the lowest production costs can offer the lowest prices and acquire the most customers. Such competition kept prices low.

Our modern economy grew up during a long period of consuming fossil fuels made cheap by their abundance. The economy adapted by applying ever more energy to solve any problem that arose. Because energy stayed cheap, consumers cared little about how efficiently they used it, like a farmer with an unlimited supply of water. Economists gave little attention to the fact that modern economies had become entirely dependent on cheap energy.

That changed in the 1970s, when the first oil shortages quadrupled the price of oil. Although the shortages were politically driven and not caused by actual depletion of resources, they still generated economic panic. Suddenly the formerly ignored issue of energy prices emerged as a crucial determinant of economic viability.

After the political turmoil subsided, energy markets settled down, and in the 1980s energy prices drifted back to historic lows. The low prices drove further growth in consumption, and even developing countries chose fossil fuels to run their economies. That's how we arrived in the 21st century with the world hooked on fossil fuels and unable to face the consequences of global warming. Cheap energy got us to this point.

How cheap? Consider your energy expense if you were tasked to hoist the Statue of Liberty five feet into the air to repair its base. The electricity consumed to drive the winch would amount to about one kilowatt-hour, which in New York City would cost you only 18 cents.[7] Even if electricity were $1 per kilowatt-hour, paying only $1 to lift the Statue of Liberty shows what an incredible bargain energy is.

The assumption that energy must remain cheap also applies to new forms of energy. For decades developers of solar and wind energy have worked to bring down the price of renewable energy low enough to compete with fossil fuels. Now that goal has largely been achieved, yet we don't have a solar-powered world. The low prices are not only not enough, they hold us back.

Cheap energy brings many drawbacks that are not helping our current situation. Cheap energy enables people and businesses to waste energy because it has little effect on their bottom line. Even when you're socially conscious enough to not waste energy, the money saved by efficiency measures hardly seems worth the effort. Making solar energy as cheap as fossil fuels will mean solar will be wasted just as much.

The push for cheap energy has also forced society to ignore the social costs of fossil fuels. Burning fossil fuels pollutes the air everyone breathes, acidifies the oceans that all marine life depends on, and induces global warming that drives catastrophic climate change around the world. The prices of fossil fuels never include these social costs. Politicians tend to veto any proposals to include social costs because that would drive up the price of energy.

Cheap energy also holds back deploying energy storage systems that would overcome the intermittent nature of solar and wind and make them as reliable as fossil fuels. Energy storage adds another cost to solar and wind, making it harder for them to compete on price alone against fossil fuels.

Every proposal for renewable energy or energy storage faces the question: "Can its price compete with fossil fuels?" The conventional answer is always "If not, then we can't use it."

Since low energy prices are holding back the transition to clean energy, it's time to reexamine that conventional wisdom. Perhaps we're trying to solve the wrong problem. A more relevant problem is how do we change the economics of energy to incentivize clean energy while maintaining a strong economy?

The pressure to keep energy cheap highlights how important energy is. Energy is the one ingredient that can make or break an economy.

That's because every aspect of every economic activity requires energy to operate. If you run a machine to extract minerals from the earth, you need energy to power that machine and transport the minerals. If you run a factory to process raw materials into finished goods, you need energy to run the machines, light the work, and move the goods. Even office work requires lighting, heating, and electricity to run the computers.

Without energy, all economic activity grinds to a halt. This becomes obvious when the power goes out to an area for an extended period. Anyone without a backup generator (which uses energy from a different source) sits idle.

We can endure such events because we know they're temporary, and we expect to get back in operation once power returns. But what if society experienced a serious extended energy shortage, such as might happen if the oil and gas industries collapsed?

Our fossil fuel industries are more fragile than you might think. They depend on financial markets to provide capital for exploration and drilling. If the financial house of cards overextends and then topples, oil and gas operations could be starved of capital and production would fall.

Gas stations would quickly run out of fuel, so the only vehicles on the road would be solar-charged electric cars. More seriously, trucks could no longer deliver food to supermarkets, where most people in cities get their food. Food production itself would halt, because farmers couldn't get tractor fuel, and food processors couldn't operate their plants. The resulting starvation panic would tear society apart.

With energy so critical to our survival, why do we assign so little value to it? We treat energy like air—vital to our well-being, but supplied free to us from nature. Energy's real value emerges when supply can no longer match demand, and we see how much people are willing to pay when they scramble to get some. After a collapse, those with solar energy systems may be the only ones still operating, and their energy would command a high price.

From that perspective it seems unreal that we treat energy as just another economic commodity. We should view energy as the *principal* economic commodity, without which all other commodities can have no value. Since energy powers all economic activity, it creates the very foundation of our economy.

So how should we assign value to this essential thing?

Energy delivers value to our society not because it's rare, but because of what it does for us. We value the actions enabled by using energy. We find it valuable that energy can transport groceries home, light our rooms, run all our tools and appliances, and deliver Internet services. How do we know these things are valuable? Because we pay money for gasoline and electricity so we can have them.

Current fossil fuel prices don't reflect that value. The prices cover the cost of production and delivery, not the value generated by using the energy. If you had to walk home with your groceries, how much would you be willing to pay for transportation instead? That question unmasks the true value of using energy.

That you can pay a low price because the production costs of fossil fuels are low seems to make driving a car a real bargain. But closer examination reveals a false bargain. That's because the price doesn't include the costs to society and the environment from mining and burning fossil fuels. Those costs are hidden from your wallet, so other people and society at large pay in the form of health risks and environmental degradation.

In the narrow economic accounting of energy used today, those external costs never appear in the equation. We ignore them because they were never considered in the past, but also because it's difficult to assign a dollar value of those costs to each unit of energy. What increment of global warming cost should we assign to a given gallon of gasoline? No one can say for sure.

But neither is it accurate to say that we don't pay those external costs in some way. In the bigger picture, real-world accounting demands we consider them. Our practice of ignoring the true cost of energy has produced our current impasse that prevents us from taking action on climate change.

Some studies have attempted to assess the full value of solar energy by including benefits to utility companies (avoided costs) and environmental benefits. For example, the US state of Maine's Public Utilities Commission determined that rooftop solar energy was actually worth 33.7 cents per kilowatt-hour when some of those benefits were included.[8]

If we take into account all external costs and benefits, solar energy would emerge with greater value than fossil fuels. Just imagine how much fossil fuels would cost if we included their negative impacts in their price. Those costs should include at least:

- The costs of relocating and compensating residents of low-lying islands and coastal areas being destroyed by rising sea levels driven by global warming.
- The costs of relocating and compensating farmers in all countries where droughts caused by climate change have destroyed their livelihood.
- The costs of repair from damage by hurricanes and typhoons induced by warmer oceans.
- The costs of health care for all those affected by air pollution from fossil fuels.
- The costs of removing the excess carbon dioxide from the atmosphere before global warming grows beyond our control.
- The costs of neutralizing the acidification of the oceans caused by excess carbon dioxide being absorbed into sea water.
- The costs of cleaning up groundwater contaminated by fracking for fossil fuels, and rivers contaminated by spills of toxic coal ash.
- The costs of military operations by all nations involved in defending oil supplies in the Middle East.

If all these very real but hidden costs were included in the price of fossil fuels, then that price would balloon beyond all precedent. Solar energy should compete against that all-inclusive high price, not the current artificially low price.

Fossil fuel prices continue to leave out those external costs while we try to force solar energy prices to match fossil fuel prices. That targets an unfair low price, brought about by an illogical economic system that allows fossil fuels to cheat, by inflicting harm on the world without compensating the world for that harm.

Solar energy carries greater value to society because it avoids all the costs we collectively pay for the negative consequences of fossil fuels. The price of solar energy should reflect its greater value. That's how we can justify a higher price for solar electricity. It is simply worth more.

Solar kilowatt-hours generated for solar dividends add more value by helping solve the three great problems we face today: global poverty, global warming, and global energy supply. A higher price for such solar power doesn't add cost arbitrarily: it pays for improving most people's lives, in this generation and all generations to come.

Some economists may label the extra cost that pays for solar dividends as a kind of tax, because it is government mandated and because it is an increment higher than the market price. Even though it is not collected and distributed by the government, it can be seen as the political and economic equivalent of a tax.

But this method of collecting money for solar dividends differs from regular taxes in several ways.

- This tax is returned to people directly as solar dividends.
- It is fair because everyone who uses energy pays it, regardless of how well they can dodge paying income taxes.

- You have some control over how much you pay, because you pay in proportion to your energy use. With tiered electricity pricing, low users pay little and high users pay much more.
- It is a separate money stream that cannot be repurposed to other government expenses.
- It is a highly cost-effective tax, with little overhead and waste because the money does not go through a government process of collection, budgeting, and disbursement.

The solar dividend program distributes that extra value to all people. Energy may cost more than it did with fossil fuels, but the benefits reach everyone, not just oil sheiks and utility shareholders.

With fossil fuels, the lucky few owning the land with deposits of coal, oil and gas get rich, while passing on all the harmful external costs of the fossil fuels to everyone else. With solar dividends, the costs are fully accounted for up front, but the benefits are distributed to all. No one gets rich, but everyone gets a share.

CHAPTER 12

Toward a Fair Economy

SOLAR DIVIDENDS HOLD OUT a promise of a better world, a world that abandons no one into poverty, a world where everyone's energy supply is local and secure, and a world where global warming and climate change are finally being brought under control.

We can accomplish all this without Draconian laws, massive "moonshot" tax expenditures, political movements, or revolution. We just have to pay gradually higher utility bills.

How could such tremendous worldwide benefits emerge from something so simple? Follow this chain of events:

1. Higher utility bills generate more revenue for utility companies.
2. Greater revenue allows utilities to purchase solar electricity at high feed-in rates.
3. The high feed-in rates create an incentive for co-ops to install solar panels.
4. Co-op solar panels generate money to pay solar dividends, which everyone will want.

5. Because everyone wants solar dividends, co-ops will install massive numbers of panels to meet the demand.
6. The massive numbers of solar panels will eventually generate enough energy to power our entire economy.[1]
7. With our economy powered by solar energy, we can abandon fossil fuels and cut the release of carbon dioxide that's the primary driver of climate change.

The price to pay for all these gains? Higher utility bills. Anyone who thinks fixing poverty, climate change, and energy supply would cost nothing is not being realistic.

The price of energy goes up, but then does not keep going up. It levels off once we completely build out the solar dividend program and enroll everyone, because solar will never experience a resource scarcity to further drive up the price. Once we adjust to higher prices, we can settle down for the long haul.

At that point, the cost of energy will be a higher percentage of the cost of goods and services than today. This will be a one-time but long overdue adjustment that resets the value that energy provides to our economy.

If fossil fuel prices go up, the solar profit margin can grow along with higher overall energy prices. Fossil fuel prices are likely to go up for two reasons, one unintentional and one intentional.

The unintentional reason comes from the declining quality of the remaining fossil fuel deposits. The energy consumed in the process of extracting fossil fuels has been growing because we've depleted the easiest deposits, and the leftovers are more difficult to produce. Now oil no longer gushes out of the ground, so oil drillers must resort to fracking to flush the oil out of tight deposits, or steaming to release it from tar sands.

Some energy economists predict the end of cheap fossil fuels will come not because we run out, but because the net energy declines too far.[2] If the extraction process consumes as much energy as is extracted, then what is the point of extracting it? Many oil and gas fields will close, overall production will fall, and demand for the remaining supplies will drive prices up.

The other reason prices may go up will come from a tax imposed on carbon. A carbon tax would intentionally raise the price of all fossil fuels to discourage carbon emissions that drive climate change, and to partially compensate for the hidden social costs that fossil fuels have always gotten away with. A carbon tax has emerged as an easy-to-administer and effective incentive for reducing carbon emissions.

In the U.S., the nonpartisan 2019 *Economists' Statement on Carbon Dividends* signed by twenty-seven Nobel Laureate economists and all living former Chairs of the Federal Reserve calls for a slowly rising carbon tax to reduce emissions.[3] Even oil giant ExxonMobil agrees to a carbon tax. In 2018 they donated $1 million to support efforts to develop carbon taxes.[4]

At this fork in our path to the future, continuing on the current fossil fuel path will see a market- or tax-driven surge in energy prices that leaves us stuck in a future with machinery still burning expensive and declining fossil fuels. The alternative solar path described here will see an equivalent but planned rising of energy prices that delivers to us an energy system that's sustainable and clean. Both paths will lead to higher energy prices, but the solar dividends path will generate far less trauma and risk, and leave us in a good position to carry on into the future.

Beyond just economics

If you review this proposal for solar dividends and you respond by just complaining about higher utility bills, then you aren't seeing the big picture.

In the big picture, energy advances from being just a cheap consumer commodity to serving as a tool to lever everyone up and out of poverty and economic insecurity. Energy changes from an economic asset worth going to war over, to a movement that can unify the world. This larger role of energy will seem new and will take time to get used to.

But it harkens back to humanity's earliest use of energy—fire. Hunter-gatherer bands congregated around a shared fire for warmth and light, creating the bonds of a strong community.

In contrast, no one designed the distribution of benefits from fossil fuels. Legal systems assumed existing land ownership laws included the ownership of new resources discovered beneath the surface. The lucky few landowners reaped great wealth from a gift of nature.

With solar energy we can design a distribution system based on the principle that everyone has a right to a share of the planet's energy income. An economy that shares energy wealth with everyone can form the basis of a unified, egalitarian, and more peaceful world. Here are five specific reasons that kind of society can develop.

1. We include all people.

This plan includes all people, regardless of their economic background, gender, political party, race, religion, or nationality. Not everyone can sign up at once because of the physical limitations of installing enough solar hardware, but after two generations, everyone can be included.

2. Each person contributes to the economy.

Every person's stake in a ten-kilowatt PV system contributes energy, the necessary animus for running an economy.

3. Each person is supported by the economy.

Unlike oil wealth reserved only for a few, the wealth generated by a solar-powered economy supports everyone through solar dividends.

4. National boundaries no longer separate us.

The sharing of solar energy and its wealth can reach people in all nations. While taking nothing away from national sovereignty, the people of the world will be unified at least by their joint participation in making solar energy. Nations will no longer need to fight each other over access to oil because every nation will generate energy within its own borders.

5. Quality of life improves.

The research to date on unconditional basic incomes finds significant improvements in the quality of life of participants. For example, when the Eastern Band of Cherokees distributed casino revenues to tribal families, researchers noted improved nutrition, higher school attendance and test scores, and reduced crime and alcoholism.[5]

In Finland, surveys of those participating in the recent test of basic incomes found: "Those in the test group experienced significantly fewer problems related to health, stress and ability to concentrate than those in the control group," the researchers wrote. "Those in the test group were also considerably more confident in their own future and their ability to influence societal issues than the control group."[6]

I believe in a future where the value of your work is not determined by the size of your paycheck, but by the amount of happiness that you spread, and the amount of meaning you give. I believe in a future where the point of education is not to prepare you for another useless job, but for a life well lived. I believe in a future where an existence without poverty is not a privilege, but a right we all deserve.

—Rutger Bregman, historian and author of
Utopia for Realists[7]

CHAPTER 13

Organizing for Solar Dividends

THE GOAL OF THIS book is not to inflict higher utility rates on everyone, but to create a way to support everyone on the planet with solar energy. That higher principle will remain a utopian dream unless we develop specific paths to achieve it. The program of solar dividends described in this book is one such path, and this chapter describes how to develop it. The chapter also covers variations that may be necessary if high feed-in rates meet too much resistance.

Solar dividends differ in so many ways from other basic income plans that we will need to create new organizations to manage them.

A full-scale implementation of solar dividends will need long-lived institutions to manage dividend payments over the life of each individual. Such institutions would secure sites for solar farms, build arrays, manage the relationship with the local utility, and make dividend payments. Because the institutions handle money, they need to be trustworthy.

The institutions will need procedures to prevent fraud. Solar dividends should only go to real people—no Internet sign-ups with fake identities, no organizations (legal or otherwise), and no government bodies.

The following sections describe three approaches to managing solar dividend programs: government run, community run, or a hybrid.

Government owned and operated

A government at any level could start a program for solar dividends. Governments exist to manage activities that benefit everyone but that no individual would take on, such as building and maintaining roads. Building and maintaining publicly owned solar farms might be new, but not that different. Governments are stable, long-lived institutions that are already managing and spending money collected as taxes.

A solar dividend program can work at any level of government because solar energy is modular. A small town can have a single solar farm while a nation would need many. The jurisdiction of a government—city, county, state/province, or nation—would determine the population eligible to receive benefits. The more local the government, the more people will feel connected to their shared ownership of the solar farms. They know that the solar farms they see every day benefit the people they see every day.

If the governing body initiating the program also regulates local utility rates, they could directly mandate higher feed-in rates for solar farms built for generating solar dividends.

The program would align with many of the existing goals of a government. Reducing poverty and transitioning people off of welfare lie within the purview of most governments. Solar dividends are not meant to replace existing welfare programs, but to prevent individuals from falling into hardship in the first place by helping them be more economically self-sufficient.

Governments should also recognize the economic benefits of local job creation and local energy production. Solar dividends spent on goods and services strengthen business activity in general, offsetting the higher energy prices that businesses will face. The Roosevelt Institute ran an economic computer simulation that showed how unconditional basic income payments would grow an economy due to the stimulative effects of the cash transfers.[1]

Governments at every level can also support solar dividends to meet their climate goals. National governments would get credit toward meeting their commitments to the Paris Climate Accord. Many state and local governments also lead efforts to reduce carbon emissions in their jurisdictions. By investing in a solar dividend program, governments would double the impact of their spending by achieving both poverty reduction and climate-change goals.

In theory, citizens trust their elected government with money. However, in many places in the world government corruption siphons off money that should benefit citizens. And even without corruption, any revenue stream collected by a government will always be subject to diversion to other budget items, undermining the reliability of the dividends.

A government-run program would need to manage its citizens' expectations for solar dividends. During the first few years, the solar income pays off the construction costs, and so produces no solar dividends. Also, the program couldn't reach all citizens immediately simply because it will take time to build out enough solar for everyone.

A government program would have to decide which distribution model to use. The model described here, where each ten-kilowatt section is dedicated to an individual, lets it achieve basic income payments large enough to change people's lives, but not everyone would be included during the first years. This approach might be more acceptable to the public if low-income people are supported first, rather than a random selection by lottery.

The alternative approach divides all solar dividends equally among all citizens. At first, payments won't amount to much, which might make the program appear trivial. But the dividends will grow over time as more solar farms are set up. This approach has the advantage of making everyone in the jurisdiction feel included because they "own" part of the solar hardware, even if the benefits are not great at first. Support for installing more publicly owned solar farms would be high since everyone could anticipate additional financial gains.

The Alaska Permanent Fund illustrates how a small but universal dividend generates support across the political spectrum. In 2019 the Alaska legislature again sought to balance the budget by using money from the Permanent Fund, reducing the individual dividends. The new governor of Alaska, far-right Christian conservative Mike Dunleavy, fought to return the annual dividend to its full amount.[2]

Community-Based Cooperatives

Because solar dividends don't come from income tax money, a government need not administer them. A private corporation could manage it, but corporations maximize profits for shareholders, where the goal here is to maximize the benefits to dividend recipients.

Cooperatives can better meet the goals of solar dividends. A cooperative operates like a business, but one controlled by its members. Co-ops maximize benefits to their members, not profits for shareholders.

Co-ops fit into the current economic system because they operate like other businesses. They're legal institutions with bylaws that describe their purpose and management. They usually have a board of directors and a staff, all of whom answer to the membership. The staff hires employees, buys goods and services in the marketplace as needed, and lines up insurance for their arrays. Co-op balance sheets are open to members, who can review them to make sure the co-op is acting in the best interests of its members.

Co-ops that manage energy aren't new. Rural electrical cooperatives have been operating continuously in the United States since the 1930s. Some co-ops generate power for their members, while others act as distributors of power purchased from electricity wholesalers. Because co-ops focus on member interests, rural electrical co-ops charge some of the lowest utility rates in the U.S.

A cooperative set up for solar dividends would dedicate itself to managing solar farms to generate dividends for members. Because the members benefit from higher dividend payments, it's in the members' interest to oversee the co-op managers to ensure efficient operation. Members would also feel a pride of ownership and a sense of belonging to a community-based system that helps people, with the added bonus of helping the environment.

A co-op's founders would choose between the two distribution methods for solar dividends when writing the co-op charter. Equally dividing all solar revenue among all members is fair, but has the disadvantage of diluting the payments if there are too many members relative to the size of the solar farms managed by the co-op. However, it would spur members to pursue development of more solar installations to raise the payments.

A co-op could instead set the membership limit to match the number of ten-kilowatt sections in the co-op's solar farms. The co-op assigns to each member a designated ten-kilowatt section, which ensures that solar dividends are of sufficient size to be useful in reducing poverty. The co-op adds members by adding additional ten-kilowatt increments.

In either method, the co-op would own the solar equipment and distribute the revenue it generates. The co-op maintains the hardware to keep it running optimally and replaces parts as needed.

If a member moves away from the area, they don't lose the annuity from their assigned 10-kW array. Because the member receives income, not electricity or goods, they can receive that income wherever they move. The co-op could automate payments through wire transfers to bank accounts. These days, even residents of rural African villages without banking services can receive payments on their mobile phones.

When a co-op member dies, their array is not subject to inheritance because the member doesn't own it. Instead, the co-op reassigns it to the next new member on the waiting list.

Local co-ops could band together into regional associations to provide mutual support. Technical and financial assistance would flow down to the co-ops from the regional associations, and practical field experience would flow up from the co-ops for wider distribution. This idea of co-op associations could grow to encompass the entire world. A World Solar Cooperative would enable the effort to cross national boundaries.[3]

Hybrid combination of government and co-ops

Although solar dividends don't require a government, one could still take part. Perhaps the most effective approach would be for a government to partner with a nongovernmental co-op. The co-op takes the leading role to build and manage solar farms for solar dividends, while a government provides support and oversight.

Such a hybrid organization would resemble a Community Action Agency (CAA) in the United States. The US government charters a CAA as a partnership between a specific government agency and a nonprofit organization for the purpose of fighting poverty. Over 1,000 CAAs in the U.S. receive funding from national, state, and local governments, as well as foundations and private donations. Since CAAs promote self-sufficiency, a government might find partnering with a similar community solar dividends co-op as a cost-effective way to meet its long-term poverty-reduction goals.

This hybrid arrangement brings several advantages. Governments would see their regional economy boosted by generating energy locally, by the reduction in poverty of their citizens, and by the local spending of solar dividends. By supporting a co-op, a government can also pursue their climate goals.

A government can play several roles to facilitate solar dividends. One important role would be to license and regulate solar co-ops. By establishing a framework of rules and regulations within which a co-op must operate, a government can protect members from unscrupulous operators.

The office that regulates co-ops could also provide information and guidance for starting a community solar co-op. The office might serve as a repository for previous case histories of other solar co-ops and provide a list of contacts to facilitate networking of information.

Governments can work with utility regulators to make sure regulations don't exclude or inhibit cooperative solar farms from competing with investor- or utility-funded solar farms. They might even help co-ops buy existing commercial solar farms to incorporate into the solar dividend program.

Governments could take a further step and develop *microgrids*, "islands" within an electrical grid that manage their own resources. Here's how the Institute for Local Self-Reliance defines them:

> Microgrids: A group of interconnected loads and distributed energy resources within clearly defined electrical boundaries that acts as a single controllable entity with respect to the grid and that connects and disconnects from the grid to enable it to operate in both grid-connected or island mode.
>
> —Institute for Local Self-Reliance[4]

For example, military bases often operate as microgrids so they can isolate themselves and keep running if the main grid fails. Community microgrids can build on existing distribution lines and equipment, connecting multiple users in a neighborhood. If there's a power outage, they offer energy independence through local power generation and distribution. Microgrids support clean energy resources such as solar, wind, and energy storage, thereby improving the environmental and economic health of the community.[5]

As a demonstration project, San Diego Gas & Electric converted the town of Borrego Springs in southern California to a microgrid starting in 2010. The microgrid encompasses rooftop solar arrays, battery energy storage, a 26-megawatt utility-scale solar array, and diesel generators as energy sources. Smart meters coordinate energy use among producers and consumers within the microgrid. In 2012, Borrego Springs became the first microgrid in the United States to rely heavily on its own solar energy and storage during a planned outage.[6]

In many locations, policies and regulations written prior to the advent of distributed solar panels and wind generators can cripple microgrids. Utility companies, which have always operated as monopolies for electricity generation and distribution, often resist the forming of microgrids. Government regulators can step in to grease the skids.

Governments can also aid co-op solar farms by leasing them land, such as highway medians and airport buffer zones. For example, a solar farm on land at the Indianapolis International Airport operates 17.5 megawatts of PV panels, a size that would support 1,750 people receiving solar dividends. The Stafford Hill Solar Farm in Vermont operates on the site of the closed Rutland City Landfill.

Alternatives to high feed-in rates

The multiple benefits of the solar dividends program, as with most good things, do not come for free. They come at the cost of gradually rising utility bills and government intervention to mandate high feed-in rates for those kilowatt-hours dedicated to solar dividends.

I've argued that this approach would be more effective than raising income taxes to pay for basic incomes, and more effective than international treaties for reducing carbon emissions. By being modular, solar dividends can also operate at any level.

But an ideal implementation may not be achievable. As with any change, solar dividends will likely meet resistance, possibly from three sources: consumers, energy interests, and economists.

Consumers will object to any increase in energy costs, because energy is a necessary expense for everyone. Witness the "yellow vest" movement in France which began in 2018 as a protest against motor fuel price increases imposed by the government (the movement has since branched into many other issues).

The solar dividends program needs to make clear that electricity prices will rise very gradually, imperceptibly at first. Also, two-thirds of the eventual burden will be borne by commercial and industrial electricity consumers, reducing the impact on individuals. For those receiving solar dividends, the extra cost is far less than their dividend. Only individuals not in the program will feel the cost without the benefit, and that will create greater urgency to complete the rollout to everyone. Businesses will feel the full cost, but they can pass the increase through in the prices of their goods and services.

The second source of resistance will come from fossil fuel interests, who have demonstrated they will fight against replacing their products with solar energy. Solar dividends will not be taking on this fight alone; there is a worldwide movement to halt climate change by shifting off of fossil fuels. Solar dividends opens up yet another front in that fight and will have many allies.

The third source of resistance will come from economists who worry that any regulation of the free market in energy will have more negative consequences than positive. One objection concerns inflation when commerce and industry pass through their extra energy expenses. There will indeed be a period of adjustment as the value of energy relative to other inputs increases. However, the impact will be very slow because these are not sudden price spikes but gradual and predictable rate increases. Because energy constitutes only a fraction of the costs that go into a product or service, prices will only go up by that fraction. Other energy trends that make energy prices volatile will also be in play during the rollout, making it hard to separate the effects of solar dividends.

Another concern is that a nation raising utility rates for solar dividends will be less competitive than nations that don't. It remains to be seen if the economic gains from massive solar construction, people with more money to spend, and fewer energy dollars draining out of the country will offset that concern.

What happens if we can't get high feed-in rates for solar dividends?

We could start anyway, by accepting the current low feed-in rates. The economics of solar dividends would change in two ways: the payback period for the solar hardware would be longer, and the monthly solar dividends would be smaller. Overhead costs would be a larger percentage and would have to be managed carefully.

Such a program would at least demonstrate to the public how it works, how they gain from it personally, and how their community is working together to reduce their carbon footprint. The dividends would be more like the Alaska Permanent Fund payments, which are too low for a basic income, but high enough to supplement working incomes and generate broad public support.

Another alternative approach would combine a carbon tax with solar dividends. A gradually rising carbon tax would raise the price of carbon-emitting electricity. If we price the solar dividend feed-in rate just below that, solar would be competitive and hence more desirable.

The revenue collected from the carbon tax could be used initially to offset part of the utility bill increases. When carbon tax revenues decline as fossil fuels phase out, the solar buy-in rates would increase to maintain the program. Governments could also choose to use carbon tax revenue to build municipally owned solar farms to generate solar dividends. That way the carbon tax serves climate change goals in two ways: it discourages fossil fuels by raising their prices, and it funds the solar replacements for fossil fuels to eliminate the carbon entirely.

Countries reluctant to impose a carbon tax could instead redirect the subsidies they currently give to fossil fuels. Worldwide, several trillion dollars could be made available to support solar dividends instead.[7] Shifting the subsidies would likely raise the price of fossil fuels, making solar even more competitive.

Solar dividends that are not big enough to generate an entire basic income can still play a part in a suite of basic income sources. Peter Barnes, founder of Working Assets Money Fund, proposes raising money for basic incomes by taxing corporations for using and often abusing our commonly shared natural wealth that includes water, air, and the electromagnetic spectrum.[8] US Presidential candidate Andrew Yang would fund basic incomes by enacting a Value-Added Tax (VAT) on all goods and services and a Financial Transaction Tax on all stock trades.[9] Economist Thomas Piketty has advocated for taxes on wealth assets (as opposed to income) to compensate for growing inequality.[10]

Combining multiple funding sources would put less burden on any single source and create greater resilience to changing economic circumstances.

International projects

The United Nations has already voiced support for basic incomes and could propagate the idea around the world. The Secretary-General of the United Nations, António Guterres, told the UN General Assembly: "The very nature of work will change. The governments may have to consider stronger social safety nets, and eventually Universal Basic Income."[11]

Many UN agencies would find that solar dividends fit into their charters for economic or energy development. For developing countries with little money to invest, the UN could coordinate wealthy individuals and nations to fund co-ops as a development aid. Such help would build lasting institutions that evolve to become self-funding through their solar income.

Poor rural villages pose particular challenges. Worldwide, about one billion people living in such villages have no basic electricity service. These villages would benefit from electricity for pumping water, lighting schools and homes so children can study at night, and refrigerating food and medicines. But many villages can't afford the electrical appliances, let alone PV panels to power them.

Consider a rural village in Kenya. Solar panels installed in the village couldn't generate much income, because people there lack the cash to buy the electricity. An indirect approach might work better in the early stages. A project could install the first ten-kilowatt PV arrays in big cities like the capital Nairobi, where electricity infrastructure is already in place, reliable electricity has a high value, and businesses and residents can afford to buy the solar electricity. Once a city-based PV array has paid itself back, the project could assign the solar income to individuals in a rural village. After several people receive their assigned systems, a steady stream of income would bootstrap the village out of poverty so it could afford water pumps, lights, and PV arrays within the village.

Delivery of money to the village requires care so that it's not diverted or misused. Many such villages already have women's co-ops for managing resources, improving education, and helping with business startups. A solar co-op in the city could pass the payments and technical help to such village co-ops. The income would help individuals install their own solar panels in the village. Over time, the co-op could build enough solar for the entire village, avoiding the need to bring in power lines from a centralized fossil fuel power plant. The local solar energy establishes a reliable and sustainable foundation for the village economy.

This example illustrates how the basic idea of solar dividends can adapt to local conditions. Different countries will have different legal and regulatory frameworks to work within. The programs will also see economic and cultural differences that determine how people can work together and handle money. A common requirement should be to manage money in a manner open to review by all co-op members to ensure fairness.

This example also highlights an innovative feature of solar dividends—the solar panels need not be located where the recipients live. The project can place the panels where the electricity market and solar conditions are best, because only the money is transferred. This option adds exceptional flexibility to the program.

Doubtless many challenges will arise in getting solar dividends working around the world to deliver reliable basic income payments from solar energy. The ubiquitous availability of solar energy enables projects to start almost anywhere by engaging local talent and ideas. Building the program from the ground up rather than top-down will root it in each community, giving it a greater chance to succeed.

CHAPTER 14

Start with a Pilot Project

EVEN THOUGH THE PROJECTED benefits of the solar dividend program are world changing, we can't expect instant adoption because no one has ever carried out such a program. Starting from where we are today, how can we create a future that includes solar dividends? We need to take two steps.

Step 1: Convince government bodies that regulate utility rates to establish a high feed-in price for solar electricity produced for a solar dividend program.

Step 2: Organize co-ops to build solar farms that generate solar dividends for individuals.

The first step, raising solar feed-in rates, is the most difficult. The second step, generating solar dividends, will follow as a natural consequence of the first step once the high feed-in rates are in place.

This plan faces a classic "chicken and egg" problem. Regulators won't raise feed-in rates for a program that does not yet exist, but the program can't exist until regulators raise rates.

They need convincing that the social benefits outweigh the social costs.

Regulators will expect pushback for forcing people and businesses to pay higher utility bills to cover the higher feed-in rates. They could only justify such increases if the social benefits can be persuasively demonstrated.

The most credible proof would be a real working project done on a small scale. A pilot program with solar arrays set up for a few people could show how solar dividends work and how individuals benefit. Such a test bed would also flag any problems that would need fixing before the program scales up.

Even a small pilot project would productively demonstrate the idea. The modular design—one ten-kilowatt array matched to one person—works for any number of participants. Ten solar arrays (100 kilowatts total) could fund ten solar dividends, while 1,000 systems (10 megawatts total) would fund 1,000 solar dividends. Each of the ten or each of the thousand recipients receives the same benefits, undiluted by the project size. A larger project could cover a wider range of people living in rich and poor circumstances, and so develop a more accurate assessment of the effects of a more universal basic income.

The most direct approach for a pilot project is to convince a utility company to participate voluntarily. The utility would make a contract with a solar co-op to pay $1 per kilowatt-hour for any solar electricity dedicated to solar dividends. Although this is a high rate for a utility to purchase electricity, it would only apply to a tiny fraction of the electricity they buy during the pilot phase. Since most of the electricity is still at the old low rates, the weighted average cost to consumers wouldn't change noticeably.

Perhaps the best candidate utility is an electric cooperative. Hundreds of electric utility cooperatives operate in the U.S. and around the world today. They deliver electric service to their customer-members, and all profits are reinvested or delivered to members. Since they focus on providing benefits to their members, they may be more receptive to a solar dividends pilot program paying cash benefits to their members.

Some electric co-ops are already connecting their members to solar. For example, the Blue Ridge Electric Membership Corporation, started in 1936 in North Carolina, now offers their members subscriptions to solar electricity generated by the co-op's community solar farms.[1] If a high feed-in rate were available, they could convert those into solar dividend farms.

A second approach to a pilot program for solar dividends would be a government mandate. If a government or utility regulatory body wanted to test the waters, they could require their utility to support a pilot program. A few systems would not significantly affect the rates their utility customers would pay. Yet the few recipients assigned to those ten-kilowatt systems would feel the full force of the feed-in rates if they each receive a $1,000 solar dividend every month.[2]

With a government mandate guaranteeing the high feed-in rate for a set number of years, a solar farm could borrow the money to install the solar panels with less risk. The first few years of income would pay off the loan, and then the solar dividends would begin. They could shorten the study period by paying all the installation costs so the solar dividends could begin immediately. Subsidies could come in the form of foundation or government money, or donations of hardware and installations by solar companies.

A third approach would be to fake utility participation and use private money to pay the difference between an existing low utility feed-in rate and the higher dividend rate. For example, if the participating utility company offers only 10 cents per kilowatt-hour for solar electricity, then private money would pay the remaining 90 cents to bring the total up to $1.00 per kilowatt-hour.

That arrangement wouldn't require a financial commitment from the utility or a regulatory step by the government. The private money would be donated from a source wanting to study the effects of a solar dividend program, such as a wealthy individual, a foundation, or a crowd-funded project. The money would not be sustainable, but would only be needed for the duration of the pilot project.

This approach needs an entity such as a nonprofit organization or government agency to coordinate all the players. They would make the arrangements with the utility company, line up the sources of subsidy money, issue a Request For Proposal to potential solar farm builders, recruit recipients, oversee the solar dividend payments, manage the study of participants, and publish the results.

Similar experiments with independent payments for solar electricity outside the normal utility billing system already exist, although not for solar dividends. For example, some privately owned solar panels in Brooklyn are selling their solar electricity to their neighbors. The Brooklyn Grid project uses a block-chain system similar to Bitcoin to keep track of solar output and money transfers, all independent of the utility company.[3]

SolarCoin is another crypto currency being developed specifically to increase the social value of solar energy, "effectively providing solar panel owners with a crowd-funded feed-in rate and encouraging more people to take part" says New Scientist writer Jacob Aron.[4]

Experiments in solar dividends can start as soon as they can be organized. They don't require international cooperation, national legislation, or even utility company approval in some cases. They can take place simultaneously in many countries and communities, adapting to local circumstances as needed.

Germany might be a particular good place to host a pilot project. They already have a strong national program for renewable energy, comprehensive social welfare programs, and many existing energy cooperatives. A German nonprofit organization, *Mein Grundeinkommen*, started a crowd-funded basic income program in 2014 that funds a few dozen people.[5] The German government also started a small tax-funded basic income program in 2019 named HartzPlus for a few welfare recipients.[6] A solar dividends pilot project should fit right in.

Such pilot projects would demonstrate on a small scale all three benefits of solar dividends. The lucky few receiving the first solar dividends would have to submit to being studied (in nonintrusive ways) to determine the effects on their lives of their basic income. The new solar panels installed for the program would have their output monitored to establish their reduction in carbon emissions compared to fossil fuels.

Once the results are in from the pilot projects, they can be directly projected onto larger scale implementations. That's because the benefits scale up proportionally with the number of solar systems. If you double the solar panels generating solar dividends, you double the number of people receiving basic incomes, double the amount of sustainable energy being produced, and double the carbon savings.

Doubling becomes a powerful force if repeated enough. The classic fable on the origin of chess illustrates this power:

> When the creator of the game of chess showed his invention to the ruler of the country, the ruler was so pleased that he gave the inventor the right to name his prize for the invention. The man, who was very wise, asked the king this: that for the first square of the chessboard, he would receive one

grain of wheat, two for the second one, four on the third one, and so forth, doubling the amount each time. The ruler, arithmetically unaware, quickly accepted the inventor's offer, even getting offended by his perceived notion that the inventor was asking for such a low price, and ordered the treasurer to count and hand over the wheat to the inventor. However, when the treasurer took more than a week to calculate the amount of wheat, the ruler asked him for a reason for his tardiness. The treasurer then gave him the result of the calculation and explained that it would be impossible to give the inventor the reward.

—Wikipedia, "Wheat and chessboard problem"

The treasurer couldn't honor the request because the total amounted to eighteen quintillion grains, which would weigh over 400 billion tons, a pile larger than Mount Everest.

With solar dividends, we can stop doubling when we reach 10 billion installations of ten-kilowatt systems (100 terawatts). The solar panels would generate enough electricity to power the world and enough money to grant solar dividends to every inhabitant of Earth.

CHAPTER 15

Conclusion

SOLAR DIVIDENDS ARE A means to achieving a larger objective, that of supporting every human on Earth with our planet's primary energy source—the sun. These two quotes encapsulate the motivation for solar dividends:

> Everyone has the right to a standard of living adequate for the health and well-being of himself and of his family.
>
> —The Universal Declaration of Human Rights, Article 25.

> Without access to energy services, people are destined to live in poverty.
>
> —Adrian Bradbrook and Judith Gardam writing in *Human Rights Quarterly*.[1]

Energy is fundamental to all economic activity, so lack of energy leaves people behind. The uneven distribution of fossil fuels on our planet has built enormous inequality into our economic systems.

Solar energy gives us a unique opportunity to correct the inequality imposed by an unequal ownership of fossil fuel energy by making sure everyone has a stake in the new solar energy system. There are not enough oil wells to go around, but there is enough sunshine for everyone. If we were to start over and design an energy system to serve all of humanity instead of the fortunate few, solar energy would be the natural choice.

The sharing of solar energy is made possible by these four facts first stated in this book's introduction:

- **Solar energy is inexhaustible.**
- **Solar energy is available all over the world.**
- **Solar energy has economic value.**
- **No one owns the sun.**

Because no one owns the sun, everyone has a right to a share of the energy from the sun. That our current economic system does not yet embrace this notion should be no great surprise, because that economy was built over the last two hundred years on a foundation of private ownership of fossil fuels.

Now that old economic system is stressing the planet with global warming and ocean acidification, which in turn stress our civilization with the threat of collapse. We can survive in the long run only if we put in place new economic patterns based on carbon-free energy sources.

The program of solar dividends is one such new economic pattern. Solar panels convert the natural value contained in the sun's rays into spendable money. And solar dividends can distribute that value fairly to all citizens of Planet Earth, creating a more stable and peaceful society.

We can test this idea starting now with pilot projects as described in the previous chapter. If the pilot projects succeed as expected, the results will open the door to widespread implementation of solar dividends.

Because the full program depends on high feed-in rates for solar electricity, governments would have to mandate such rates for the electric utilities they regulate, which would result in higher utility bills for electricity users. The results of the pilot projects should give governments the data they need to overcome the inevitable resistance to raising utility rates.

They can justify taking such actions because the solar dividend program pursues three far-reaching goals:

- Rescue everyone from economic insecurity.
- Halt the release of greenhouse gases from fossil fuels.
- Build an energy system that can sustain human civilization essentially forever.

These big goals signify a better future for human society, but can solar dividends achieve such ambitious objectives?

To answer that question, consider the concrete actions we would take under this program to meet these goals:

- Build solar farms intending to earn income for solar dividends.
- Raise the utility feed-in rates for kilowatt-hours generated specifically for solar dividends.
- Pay monthly minimum incomes to everyone from the solar-generated income.

These actions are specific and realistic. Solar farms are already being built around the world, and some jurisdictions are already experimenting with setting high feed-in rates for solar electricity. We only need to create the social arrangements to reliably distribute the solar proceeds as unconditional basic incomes. No insurmountable technical or legal barriers stand in the way, so we can start immediately.

The numbers may play out differently from my working example of 10 kilowatts per person generating a $1,000 per month solar dividend from a feed-in rate of $1.00 per kilowatt-hour from the utility. Such nice round numbers serve as a starting point for discussion, but the actual numbers will differ depending on the circumstances. If we have a smaller feed-in rate, then we may need a larger array. Locations with more sunshine can use a smaller array. Countries where $1 goes further in purchasing power may not need as much as $1,000/month per person.

Obviously, we can't provide everyone with solar dividends overnight. Building enough solar farms to cover everyone will take many years, but each ten-kilowatt increment installed for solar dividends moves one person into the program. That person gains the benefits of a minimum basic income for their lifetime. That increment of solar panels also displaces an increment of fossil fuels and moves our global energy system one step closer to sustainability. We accomplish the three objectives for each increment, albeit on a small scale for each increment.

Achieving the larger goals requires repeating that pattern— add more panels in this modular fashion and gradually move more people into the program.

If we continue that process and grow the program in every country, the full impact develops as coverage expands. By 2070 we could see every person on the planet receiving a significant minimum income from solar dividends generated from a solar array somewhere in the world. That key result is measurable and verifiable, providing a clear metric for the success of the program.

This idea also fits into the current economic system, with one change—we set high feed-in rates for electricity generated for solar dividends. That change requires political will to overcome the resistance from vested interests and conventional economists who insist on free-market energy prices. But that single change will push the program into high gear by the incentive it creates.

Our current economy may not be ready for high feed-in rates. But our current economy is also unsustainable and unprepared for the future. Changes must be coming if we are to survive. You can imagine there might be room for solar dividends in an economy designed for sustainability because they provide both sustainable energy and sustainable income.

Naysayers will emerge who claim the idea won't work. But they can only criticize the implementation details, not the fundamental strength of the idea—that solar energy has economic value we can share among all people. Criticism of the details can help shape the program as long as we keep the goals in mind.

Do the goals inspire action? Perhaps the goal of reducing worldwide carbon emissions is too vast for most people to relate to. You might hear "Fixing the entire world's atmosphere is not my problem, even if I could fix it." To date, climate change has generated little popular revolt against politicians and industrialists who persist in maintaining our fossil fuel energy system.

But people are concerned about their economic well-being. The goal of providing basic incomes for yourself, your children, and all your descendants can inspire individual engagement. Everyone can relate to improving personal economic security, reducing their own risk of homelessness, and expanding opportunities for their children. Ask yourself: if your children were offered such a program, would you sign them up?

We can mobilize the desire for economic security as an indirect means to achieve the goals of climate stability and energy sustainability. By recruiting solar energy as a new mechanism to fund basic incomes, we see basic incomes become a new reason to install more solar energy. Combining these two big ideas provides the inspiration to pursue this program.

Those seeking a quick fix to our world problems should look elsewhere. Solar dividends provide a long-term plan to build a better world, a plan that we can carry out incrementally and methodically. The benefits emerge at the pace we apply it.

Powerful economic forces will try to maintain the status quo. My purpose is not to fight those powerful interests, but to replace them in the long run.

> You never change things by fighting the existing reality. To change something, build a new model that makes the existing model obsolete.
>
> —R. Buckminster Fuller

This vision of a solar-powered world distributing solar dividends to everyone could become such a new model. Making this new model a reality is the challenge of our time.

Humanity is just now awakening to the value of solar energy. Grounding this effort on the principle that no one owns the sun, there's no fundamental reason why the economic value of solar energy can't be shared among all people. If we keep this larger principle in mind, we can push through the minutia of implementing solar dividends. If we want this future, I believe we can figure out how to bring it about.

It seems to me that our problem has a lot less to do with the mechanics of solar power than the politics of human power—specifically whether there can be a shift in who wields it, a shift away from corporations and toward communities, which in turn depends on whether or not the great many people who are getting a rotten deal under our current system can build a determined and diverse enough social force to change the balance of power.

—Naomi Klein, *This Changes Everything: Capitalism vs. the Climate*

You may say I'm a dreamer,
but I'm not the only one.

—John Lennon

Part B: Building That Future

Appendix A. Do The Numbers Add Up?

This appendix is for those who like the idea of solar dividends but won't be convinced until they see the numbers. It tries to answer the following questions:

1. How big are solar dividends?
2. Why won't utility bills go up quickly?
3. How much solar will we need?

How big are solar dividends?

The formula for calculating a solar dividend multiplies together several factors:

Annual solar dividend (dollars) = array size (in kilowatts)
    × capacity factor (%)
    × feed-in rate (in dollars per kwh)
    × economic efficiency (%)
    × 8760 hours/year

The factors are:

- array size: the rated capacity of solar panels, measured in kilowatts.
- capacity factor: the ratio of actual output to maximum potential output.

- feed-in rate: what the utility company pays for solar dividend electricity, in dollars per kilowatt-hour.
- economic efficiency: the percentage of the feed-in rate that reaches the recipient after subtracting overhead costs.
- 8760 hours: the number of hours in a year.

Although the panels are exposed for all 8760 hours in a year, they obviously are not producing electricity all those hours because of night and clouds. Those conditions, as well as several others, are all taken into account by the capacity factor.

The capacity factor is the ratio of actual output to maximum output for the array. The maximum electricity that an array could possibly produce would occur if the panels were aimed directly at the full sun 24 hours per day. That maximum could only be achieved if the array were out in space and always pointed at the sun. On Earth, any clouds, night hours, and the changing angles of the sun reduce the actual annual output to some fraction of the theoretical "outer space" output. That fraction is the capacity factor, expressed as a percentage. The capacity factor encapsulates in a single measure all the variability due to weather, night, seasonal sun angles, latitude, and panel setup. Capacity factors range from about 10% in high latitude or cloudy locations up to about 22% in sunny locations, with a few locations outside this range.

The base example for solar dividends in this book assumes the following numbers:

$12,009.96 annual solar dividend = 10 kilowatt array size
   × 15% capacity factor
   × $1.00 per kwh feed-in rate
   × 91.4% economic efficiency
   × 8760 hours

By adjusting these numbers, solar dividends can be as big or small as we choose to make them. To form an adequate basic income, I set the size of solar dividends at $1,000 per month, which is the same amount as US presidential candidate Andrew Yang[1] is proposing, as well as some other basic income writers such as Andy Stern.[2]

In locations with a lower capacity factor, the array size or the feed-in rate (or both) could be raised to compensate. In locations with a higher capacity factor, the array size or feed-in rate could be reduced.

For example, an array in cloudy Seattle, Washington with a capacity factor of 12.5%[3] would need to be enlarged to 12 kilowatts to generate the same solar dividend:

$12,009.96 annual solar dividend = 12 kilowatt array size
- × 12.5% capacity factor
- × $1.00 per kwh feed-in rate
- × 91.4% economic efficiency
- × 8760 hours

In all locations, a high economic efficiency needs to be maintained to ensure that the money generated reaches the recipient and is not eaten up in overhead.

Why won't utility bills go up quickly?

The strongest objection to solar dividends will likely be that electric utility bills will go up to pay for them. That's true in the long run when solar dividends support everyone, but in the early years of the program the change will hardly be noticeable. Why? Because of the pace that the solar dividend program will roll out.

The delay comes from the real-world limitations on the rate of installing solar energy systems. It's simply impossible to install enough solar hardware to deliver solar dividends to everyone immediately. It will take time to organize solar co-ops, negotiate sites, and build solar farms.

On the day that a government puts in place a $1 per kilowatt-hour feed-in rate for solar dividend electricity, what happens? Nothing, because no such electricity is being generated yet, except for any existing small-scale pilot projects.

The program has to grow from nothing to full coverage over time, and given the size of the world's population, that will take decades. People may wish it could happen overnight to respond quickly to the urgency of our climate crisis, but that is not physically or economically possible, even if it were instituted as a crash program.

The solar dividends program will follow a realistic pattern where it grows by a percentage each year. When something grows by a percentage each year, it is growing exponentially. Compound interest on a savings account with a fixed interest rate is frequently cited as an example of exponential growth. If the interest earned in one year stays in the account, then that interest earns interest during the next year, compounding the growth rate. With enough time, the accumulated interest can overtake and exceed the original amount.

Exponential growth is much faster than linear growth, because instead of growing by a fixed amount each year, it grows by a fixed percentage of the previous year. Since each year's total is bigger than the previous year's, the absolute amount added each year gets bigger. In other words, the annual growth is growing.

A graph of exponential growth always curves upward over time, simply because each year's growth is larger than the previous year's growth. The growth of the photovoltaics industry has been following an exponential pattern for decades.

Exponential Growth of Photovoltaic

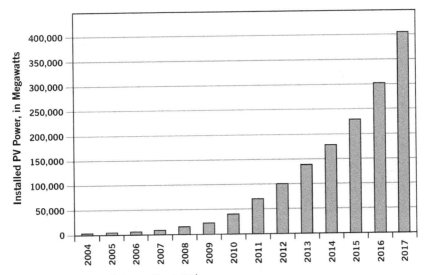

Figure 1. Exponential growth of PV[4]

Notice how in the early part of the curve the values are low relative to the later years? That's because an exponential growth pattern starts with a small base. Even if it grows by a large percentage, that change in the base looks small compared to the ultimate goal. Only in the later years when the base has grown does a percentage increase appear large on the curve.

During the early years, solar dividend co-ops will generate a tiny fraction of all electricity produced. Only those solar co-op kilowatt-hours get the high feed-in rate, while all the rest get the regular low rate. Like adding a drop of ink to a gallon of water, the high rate is diluted by the much larger number of low-rate kilowatt-hours. That dilution means utility bills in the early years will see only tiny increases.

How much solar will we need?

While I can't predict the future, I can show how a solar future is possible. I'll give you plausible numbers along with my assumptions and reasoning behind them. Because solar dividends are modular—one solar array for one person—my calculations can be done on a per capita basis. That makes them easier to relate to, and then they can be scaled up to the entire population.

Here are my assumptions:

- In the future, world population levels off at 10 billion people.
- Modern energy services are extended to the 1 billion people currently without them.
- All fossil fuels are replaced by electricity and renewable fuels generated from solar, wind and hydropower.
- Energy storage systems match the energy sources to the energy demands.
- We use energy more efficiently than we do today.
- We maintain good environmental standards while making and installing solar equipment.
- Any raw material shortages are resolved by new technologies.

If we start with the per capita energy use in a developed country, apply these assumptions, and extrapolate to the future world population, how much energy would be needed in a fully solar future?

Germany can serve as a reference case because it has a mature modern economy with a mix of industrial, commercial, residential, and transportation energy use. The average annual energy use per person in Germany was 43,800 kilowatt-hours in 2015.[5] This number counts all energy in all forms used in Germany in a year, divided by the population size. If you then divide by the number of hours in a year, you get the average per capita rate of energy use, about 5 kilowatts per person in 2015.

To clarify, a kilowatt is a *rate* at which energy is used. If you use an appliance rated at one kilowatt, it consumes energy at a rate of one kilowatt-hour per hour. So 5 kilowatts used for 24 hours would amount to 120 kilowatt-hours of energy used each day (5 times 24), and multiplying that by 365 days brings the total energy use for a year to 43,800 kilowatt-hours.

That 5 kilowatts is not a personal rate of energy use, but rather each person's share of the rate that all energy is used in the country, including industrial, commercial, and transportation energy as well as personal use.

This number needs to be adjusted in two ways for our solar future. The first adjustment is for replacing heat engines with electric motors. A heat engine is any device that converts heat to mechanical power. A car engine is a heat engine, as are power plants burning coal or natural gas. Heat engines are only 20-40% efficient, which means 60-80% of the original energy in the fossil fuels ends up as waste heat that is thrown away. We tolerate such waste today because heat engines are the only means of converting fossil fuels to electricity and motive power for transportation. Because we are replacing heat engines with electric motors, we won't experience such heat losses in the future, so we won't need as much raw energy as we use today.

Experts tabulate the world's raw energy consumption as 158,715 terawatt-hours in 2015.[6] When they subtract out the losses from heat engines, the energy in final form delivered to people was only 109,136 terawatt-hours. This difference is important because solar, along with wind and hydropower, produce electricity directly so the energy is already in its final form. Without the huge energy losses of heat engines, solar-based energy sources need to supply only the smaller number.

So we can reduce our 5 kilowatts per person by the ratio of those two numbers (0.687), which gets us down to 3.44 kilowatts. That's a 31% reduction just by replacing the burning of fossil fuels with directly-generated electricity.

The second adjustment comes from using energy more efficiently. Efficiency does not mean doing without, it means doing the same job but with less energy. Since most of our current energy-using systems developed over a period when energy was cheap, they have plenty of room to improve in their efficiency. Estimates of the potential energy savings range from 35% to 50%. If we conservatively take the low end of that range (35%), we would only need to supply 2.25 kilowatts per person.

So if we replace heat engines and become more efficient, we can provide every person in our future world with energy services equivalent to those in Germany today if we supply them an average rate of energy flow of 2.25 kilowatts.

That does *not* mean we can set up 2.25 kilowatts of solar panels to meet that need. The 2.25 kilowatts average is actually energy needed for 24 hours, and the sun does not shine 24 hours. So how much solar hardware would be needed?

Let's estimate that 25% of the world's renewable electricity supply will come from wind and hydropower, which leaves us needing only 1.68 kilowatts of electricity from PV panels. To determine the size of the solar array to meet that need, we have to estimate the capacity factor.

As described above, the capacity factor is a ratio that compares any panel's actual energy output to the energy the panel would produce if it were aimed straight at the sun twenty-four hours per day. Capacity factors for solar panels range from 10% to 22% depending on the latitude and weather at a given location. We can take the midpoint 16% as a reasonable average for the world. That's equivalent to a panel getting strong sun for about four hours per day on average.

With a 16% capacity factor, you calculate the array size by dividing our energy requirement of 1.68 kilowatts by 0.16 to get 10.5 kilowatts. In other words, a person's 10.5 kilowatt array operating at 16% capacity factor delivers an average of 1.68 kilowatts of usable energy.

To summarize, if we can get 25% of our energy from wind and hydropower, and if we install about 10 kilowatts of PV panels for each person on the planet, then we can meet all of our adjusted energy needs in the future. With 10 billion people, this would add up to 100 terawatts of PV panels.

Is 100 terawatts of solar PV outrageously high compared to other projections? We can compare these estimates with the most detailed scientific study to date of how the world could generate 100% of our energy from renewable energy sources. The study by the Lappeenranta University of Technology in Finland and the Energy Watch Group in Germany ran computer simulations of patterns of hourly consumption of all forms of energy, and matched them to a renewable energy supply that was combined with energy storage. Like my estimate, they assumed improvements in energy efficiency and extending energy services to currently underserved populations.[7]

The study found that by 2050 we could meet all human energy needs with 63 terawatts of solar PV (compared to my estimate of 100 terawatts) combined with an additional 27% coming from wind, hydropower, and biofuels. Their study had three differences from my estimate: that 27% of all energy would come from other renewable sources (compared to my 25%), a lower 9.7 billion population (compared to my 10 billion), and higher efficiency improvements of 49% (compared to my 35%). Adjusting their figure of 63 terawatts by these three factors would change their requirement to 93 terawatts of solar PV, which is within 7% of my estimate of 100 tera-watts.

Would the solar panels cover the entire planet? Installing 100 terawatts of today's solar panels would only cover a total area of 258,000 square miles, which is about the area of Texas, less than half of one percent of the world's land area. They would be scattered all over the surface of the planet, and most installations could be dual use so the original land use is retained. We would not need to cover the entire planet in solar panels.

These results confirm that if we installed an average of 10 kilowatts of PV panels for each person on the planet to generate solar dividends, we could provide that person with a basic income *and* meet the world's energy needs. I base this not on any absolute numbers predicted for 50 years in the future, but on the per capita numbers that we can apply today. The future will gauge the success of solar dividends by the degree those per capita numbers are scaled to everyone on Planet Earth.

Notes and References

Preface : A New Approach

1. The United Nations Framework Convention on Climate Change (UNFCCC) hosts annual formal meetings of the UNFCCC Parties (Conference of the Parties, COP) to assess progress in dealing with climate change. Wikipedia contributors, "United Nations Climate Change conference," Wikipedia, The Free Encyclopedia, https://en.wikipedia.org/wiki/United_Nations_Climate_Change_conference (accessed 4 August 2019).

2. DParthasarathy, "COP24: Countries struggle to muster political will to tackle climate crisis." Climate Action Network International, December 15, 2018, http://climatenetwork.org/press-release/cop24-countries-struggle-muster-political-will-tackle-climate-crisis

3. Robert J. Brulle, *Institutionalizing delay: foundation funding and the creation of U.S. climate change counter-movement organizations*, Climatic Change (2014) 122: 681. https://doi.org/10.1007/s10584-013-1018-7

4. David Coady, Ian Parry, Nghia-Piotr Le, and Baoping Shang, *Global Fossil Fuel Subsidies Remain Large: An Update Based on Country-Level Estimates*, Working Paper WP/19/89, International Monetary Fund, May 2019, https://www.imf.org/en/Publications/WP/Issues/2019/05/02/Global-Fossil-Fuel-Subsidies-Remain-Large-An-Update-Based-on-Country-Level-Estimates-46509

Chapter 2: My Story

1. Here are the numbers. The co-op deposited $1000 per month for fourteen years (age four to eighteen) with 3% annual interest compounded monthly yields $208,467.15. Figures according to https://www.bankrate.com/calculators/savings/simple-savings-calculator.aspx

2. As of 2019, semitransparent PV panels are being developed on several fronts. Gail Overton, "New solar panels harvest energy and also allow crops to grow underneath", Laser Focus World, 5 July 2018, https://www.laserfocusworld.com/articles/2018/07/new-solar-panels-harvest-energy-and-also-allow-crops-to-grow-underneath.html. Jennifer McNulty, "Solar greenhouses generate electricity and grow crops at the same time, UC Santa Cruz study reveals", University of California Santa

Cruz News Center, 3 November 2017, https://news.ucsc.edu/2017/11/loik-greenhouse.html.

3. The panels are specifically designed to absorb and convert infrared energy into electricity. Since the sun's infrared has the strongest drying effect on the land, removing the infrared greatly reduces water evaporation from the soil, leaving the water available for the growing grass. The strong infrared conversion also allowed the panels to operate at night, running off the infrared emitted by the earth underneath.

4. John Weaver, "All I want for Christmas is a 90% efficient solar panel," PV Magazine, 23 November 2108, https://pv-magazine-usa.com/2018/11/23/all-i-want-for-christmas-is-a-90-efficient-solar-panel/.

Chapter 3: Solar for Everyone

1. Since 2002, Sherman County in Oregon has been providing households with a $590 annual dividend from the property taxes generated by the wind turbines in that county. Sierra Dawn McClain, *Editorial: What Alaska and Sherman County, Ore., have in common*, Capital Press, 25 July 2019, https://www.capitalpress.com/opinion/editorials/editorial-what-alaska-and-sherman-county-ore-have-in-common/article_2fa0d9e0-a9b3-11e9-a101-6f0b2a46f5e6.html

Chapter 4: Our Solar-Powered Economy in 2099

1. Several studies predict that a 100% solar-powered world is possible, including a) Karl Burkart, *One Earth Climate Model*, Leonardo DiCaprio Foundation, June 2019, https://www.onlynaturalenergy.com/one-earth-climate-model/ b) *Global Energy System Based on 100% Renewable Energy* by Lappeenranta University of Technology in Finland and Energy Watch Group in Berlin, 2018, http://energywatchgroup.org/new-study-global-energy-system-based-100-renewable-energy c) Mark Z. Jacobson, Mark A. Delucchi, Zack A.F. Bauer, ..., Jingfan Wang, Eric Weiner, Alexander S. Yachanin, *100% Clean and Renewable Wind, Water, and Sunlight All-Sector Energy Roadmaps for 139 Countries of the World*, Joule 1, pages 108–121 September 6, 2017, Elsevier Inc. http://dx.doi.org/10.1016/j.joule.2017.07.005

2. "Oregon restricts solar development on prime farmland." Cassandra Profita, The Columbian, July 6, 2019, https://www.columbian.com/news/2019/jul/06/oregon-restricts-solar-development-on-prime-farm-land/

3. Ecological Society of America. "Solar panels cast shade on agriculture in a good way." *ScienceDaily*. https://www.sciencedaily.com/releases/2019/07/190729123751.htm (accessed July 31, 2019).

4. Rebecca R. Hernandez et al, "Techno–ecological synergies of solar energy for global sustainability", *Nature Sustainability*, Volume 2, July 2019, pp 560–568, https://www.nature.com/articles/s41893-019-0309-z.

5. Emiliano Bellini, *South Korean government announces 2.1 GW floating PV project*, PV Magazine, July 19, 2019, https://www.pv-magazine.com/2019/07/19/south-korean-government-announces-2-1-gw-floating-pv-project/

6. Javier Farfan, Christian Breyer, *Combining Floating Solar Photovoltaic Power Plants and Hydropower Reservoirs: A Virtual Battery of Great Global Potential*, 12 International Renewable Energy Storage Conference, IRES 2018, https://www.sciencedirect.com/science/article/pii/S1876610218309858

7. Taylor Briglio et al, *A Feasibility Analysis of Installing Solar Photovoltaic Panels Over California Water Canals*, UCLA Institute of the Environment and Sustainability, June 2014, https://www.slideshare.net/GrokOur-Worlds/ucla-solar-canal-feasibility-study

8. Methanol is a liquid alcohol essentially made from carbon dioxide, water, and energy. A fuel cell converts methanol back to electricity, with water and carbon dioxide as waste products. No greenhouse gases are involved, because no methane gas is produced, and the carbon dioxide that's released was originally taken from the air to make the methanol, so there's no net release of carbon dioxide. For more information on methanol for energy transport and storage, see: George A. Olah, Alain Goeppert, G. K. Surya Prakash, *Beyond Oil and Gas: The Methanol Economy*, 3rd Edition, Wiley-VCH (October 22, 2018)

9. James Ayre, *Low-Cost Methanol From Carbon Dioxide — Relatively Cheap Conversion Method Developed*, Clean Technica, 4 March 2014, https://cleantechnica.com/2014/03/04/low-cost-methanol-carbon-dioxide-relatively-cheap-conversion-method-developed/

10. Wikipedia contributors, "Hyperloop," Wikipedia, The Free Encyclopedia, https://en.wikipedia.org/wiki/Hyperloop (accessed 4 August 2019).

11. For example, see Eco Marine Power, https://www.ecomarinepower.com

12. Licht, Stuart & Wu, Hongjun & Hettige, Chaminda & Wang, Baohui & Asercion, Joseph & Lau, Jason & Stuart, Jessica. (2012). *STEP cement: Solar Thermal Electrochemical Production of CaO without CO2 emission.* Chemical communications (Cambridge, England). February 2012. https://www.researchgate.net/publication/224856443_STEP_cement_Solar_Thermal_Electrochemical_Production_of_CaO_without_CO2_emission

13. Zaldívar copper mine moves to 100% renewable power, Mining Journal, 20 July 2018, https://www.mining-journal.com/copper-news/news/1342892/zald%C3%ADvar-copper-mine-moves-to-100-renewable-power

14. Cherie Gough, "How Aquaponics, A.K.A. Fish Poop, Can Grow Food Using Less Water And Land," Huffington Post, 30 January 2019, https://www.huffpost.com/entry/aquaponics-fish-poop-food_n_5c48b7e3e4b025aa26bf6f82

Chapter 5: Carbon Emissions Under Control in 2099

1. George Foulsham, *Researchers turn carbon dioxide into sustainable concrete* Phys.org, 15 March 15 2016 https://phys.org/news/2016-03-carbon-dioxide-sustainable-concrete.html

Chapter 6: Energy Prices Went Up

1. Wikipedia contributors, "German Renewable Energy Sources Act," Wikipedia, The Free Encyclopedia, https://en.wikipedia.org/wiki/German_Renewable_Energy_Sources_Act (accessed 29 January 2019).

Chapter 7: We Adapted to Higher Energy Prices

1. This effect was discovered in the 1970s during the worst energy price jump in modern history. The price of oil rose from $3 per barrel before the 1973 Oil Embargo to $40 per barrel by 1979, over thirteen times higher, but the U.S. Consumer Price Index only doubled, from 41.2 in early 1972 to 86.3 by the end of 1980. Nick K. Lioudis, *The Relationship Between Oil Prices & Inflation*, Investopedia, June 1, 2018, https://www.investopedia.com/ask/answers/06/oilpricesinflation.asp

2. Ken Webster, *The Circular Economy: A Wealth of Flows*, Second Edition, Ellen MacArthur Foundation Publishing, 2016.

3. The Ämmässuo Waste Treatment Centre already operates in 2019 recycling 99% of what goes in, with 100% as their goal. Graham Lawton, *Towards a world without landfill*, New Scientist, 10 November 2018, https://doi.org/10.1016/S0262-4079(18)32064-5

4. William McDonough, Michael Braungart, *Cradle to Cradle: Remaking the Way We Make Things*, North Point Press, 2010. See also the Cradle to Cradle Products Innovation Institute, https://www.c2ccertified.org/

Chapter 9: Unconditional Basic Income

1. Basic Income Earth Network, *About Basic Income*, http://basicincome.org/basic-income/, 2017.

2. Ioana Marinescu, *No Strings Attached: The Behavioral Effects of U.S. Unconditional Cash Transfer Programs*, The Roosevelt Institute, May 2017, https://rooseveltinstitute.org/no-strings-attached/

3. Deborah Hardoon, *An Economy for the 99%*, Oxfam Briefing Paper, Published by Oxfam GB for Oxfam International under ISBN 978-0-85598-861-6 in January 2017, https://www.oxfam.org/en/research/economy-99

4. Jason Hickel, *The Divide: A Brief Guide to Global Inequality and its Solutions*, William Heinemann Publishing, 2017

5. Thomas Piketty, *Capital in the Twenty-First Century*, The Belknap Press of Harvard University Press, 2014.

6. Laura Spinney, "The Fall", New Scientist, 20 January 2018, https://www.newscientist.com/article/mg23731610-300-end-of-days-is-western-civilisation-on-the-brink-of-collapse/

7. *Jobs Lost, Jobs Gained: Workforce Transitions in a Time of Automation* McKinsey Global Institute, December 2017, https://www.mckinsey.com/featured-insights/future-of-work/jobs-lost-jobs-gained-what-the-future-of-work-will-mean-for-jobs-skills-and-wages

8. Martin Ford, *Rise of the Robots: Technology and the Threat of a Jobless Future*, Basic Books (May 5, 2015).

9. Guy Standing, *The Precariat: The New Dangerous Class* , Bloomsbury Academic, 2016.

10. Ibid, Martin Ford, *Rise of the Robots.*

11. Ipsos MORI, "Universal Basic Income Research," Poll Conducted for University of Bath – Institute for Policy Research, September 2017, https://www.ipsos.com/sites/default/files/ct/news/documents/2017-09/omnibus-universal-basic-income-topline-2017.pdf

12. Grace Donnelly, *Finland's Basic Income Experiment Will End in 2019*, Fortune Magazine, April 19, 2018, http://fortune.com/2018/04/19/finland-universal-basic-income-experiment-ending/

13. Luke Martinelli, *Assessing the Case for a Universal Basic Income in the UK*, IPR Policy Brief, Institute for Policy Research, Bath, UK, September 2017, https://www.bath.ac.uk/publications/assessing-the-case-for-a-universal-basic-income-in-the-uk/

14. Mark Shekin, Yale University, quoted in *The inequality delusion*, New Scientist, 31 March 2018, https://www.newscientist.com/article/mg23731710-300-the-inequality-delusion-why-weve-got-the-wealth-gap-all-wrong/

15. OECD (2017), *Basic income as a policy option: Can it add up?*, Policy Brief on The Future of Work, OECD Publishing, Paris. http://www.oecd.org/els/emp/Basic-Income-Policy-Option-2017.pdf

16. *Report of the Special Rapporteur on extreme poverty and human rights*, United Nations Human Rights Council, A/HRC/35/26, June 2017, https://www.ohchr.org/EN/Issues/Poverty/Pages/SRExtremePovertyIndex.aspx

Chapter 10: Solar Dividends as Basic Incomes

1. Howard Reed and Stewart Lansley, *Universal Basic Income: An idea whose time has come?*, A publication by Compass, London, May 2016, https://www.compassonline.org.uk/wp-content/uploads/2016/05/Universal-BasicIncomeByCompass-Spreads.pdf

2. Note that the basic income would not scale down proportionally because some overhead costs remain constant regardless of the rate, leaving less available for the dividend.

Chapter 11: The True Value of Solar Energy

1. These array sizes assume the panels are tilted up at an angle equivalent to the location's latitude and oriented true south, conditions likely to be fulfilled on a solar farm. The PVWatts calculator is available free online at https://pvwatts.nrel.gov/.

2. National Conference of State Legislatures, *State Renewable Portfolio Standards and Goals*, February 2019, http://www.ncsl.org/research/energy/renewable-portfolio-standards.aspx

3. If your utility bill was for 100 kilowatt-hours and half were at $1.00 and the other half at $.12, then 50 of those would cost $50.00 and the other fifty would cost $6.00, for an average of $.56 per kilowatt-hour.

4. Wikipedia contributors, "Electricity Pricing," Wikipedia, The Free Encyclopedia, https://en.wikipedia.org/wiki/Electricity_pricing (accessed 29 January 2019).

5. Pacific Gas & Electric Company, *Electric Schedule E-1, Residential Services*, July 2019, https://www.pge.com/tariffs/assets/pdf/tariffbook/ELEC_SCHEDS_E-1.pdf

6. One AAA alkaline battery can deliver 1.15 amp-hours at 1.5 volts. That's 1.725 watt-hours of energy, or .001725 kilowatt-hours, so the cost per kilowatt-hour is $.50 divided by .001725 = $290.

7. The Statue of Liberty weighs 450,000 pounds. Raising it 5 feet in the air requires 450,000 pounds x 5 feet = 2,250,000 foot-pounds of energy. One kilowatt-hour is equivalent to 2,655,223 foot-pounds, so if there were no loses it would require 0.847 kilowatt-hour. More realistically, if the winch and pulleys were 80% efficient in transfering the energy, that amounts to 1.06 kilowatt-hour.

8. Maine Public Utilities Commission, *Maine Distributed Solar Valuation Study*, Revised April 14, 2015, https://www.maine.gov/mpuc/electricity/elect_generation/documents/MainePUCVOS-FullRevisedReport_4_15_15.pdf

Chapter 12: Toward a Fair Economy

1. A 100% solar-powered economy is possible if energy is used more efficiently and energy storage matches the supply to demand.

2. Lambert, J. G., Hall, C. A., Balogh, S., Gupta, A., & Arnold, M. (2014). Energy, EROI and quality of life. Energy Policy, 64, 153-167, https://www.sciencedirect.com/science/article/pii/S0301421513006447

3. *Economists' Statement on Carbon Dividends*, 16 January 2019, https://www.wsj.com/articles/economists-statement-on-carbon-dividends-11547682910

4. Steven Mufson, "ExxonMobil gives $1 million to promote a carbon tax-and-dividend plan," Washington Post 9 October 2018, https://www.washingtonpost.com/energy-environment/2018/10/09/exxon-mobil-gives-million-promote-carbon-tax-and-dividend-plan/

5. Ioana Marinescu, *No Strings Attached: The Behavioral Effects of U.S. Unconditional Cash Transfer Programs*, The Roosevelt Institute, May 2017, https://rooseveltinstitute.org/no-strings-attached/

6. Emma Charlton, *The results of Finland's basic income experiment are in. Is it working?*, World Economic Forum, 12 February 2019, https://www.weforum.org/agenda/2019/02/the-results-finlands-universal-basic-income-experiment-are-in-is-it-working/

7. Rutger Bregman, *Poverty isn't a lack of character; it's a lack of cash*, TED Talk, TED2017, April 2017, https://www.ted.com/talks/rutger_bregman_poverty_isn_t_a_lack_of_character_it_s_a_lack_of_cash

Chapter 13: Organizing for Solar Dividends

1. Michalis Nikiforos, Marshall Steinbaum, and Gennaro Zezza, *Modeling the Macroeconomic Effects of a Universal Basic Income*, Roosevelt Institute, August 2017, https://rooseveltinstitute.org/modeling-macroeconomic-effects-ubi/

2. *Why a conservative Alaskan Governor promotes a Universal Basic Income*, Basic Income Today, April 2019, https://basicincometoday.com/why-a-conservative-alaskan-governor-promotes-a-universal-basic-income/5258

3. There exists a Global Basic Income Foundation based in The Netherlands whose goal is to grant a basic income for all people on the planet. Their proposals are currently based on taxes, not solar energy.

4. Matt Grimley and John Farrell, *Mighty Microgrids*, Institute for Local Self-Reliance, March 2016, https://ilsr.org/report-mighty-microgrids/

5. *Microgrids 101*, New York State Energy Research and Development Authority, https://www.nyserda.ny.gov/All-Programs/Programs/NY-Prize/Resources-for-applicants/Microgrids-101

6. *Microgrids Help Integrate Renewable Energy and Improve Community Resiliency*, San Diego Gas & Electric, https://www.sdge.com/more-information/environment/smart-grid/microgrids

7. Richard Bridle, Shruti Sharma, Mostafa Mostafa, Anna Geddes, *Fossil Fuel to Clean Energy Subsidy Swaps:How to pay for an energy revolution*, Global Studies Initiative, International Institute for Sustainable Development, 2019, https://www.iisd.org/library/fossil-fuel-clean-energy-subsidy-swap

8. Peter Barnes, *With Liberty and Dividends for All: How to Save Our Middle Class When Jobs Don't Pay Enough*, Berrett-Koehler Publishers; 1 edition (August 4, 2014).

9. Andrew Yang, *The War on Normal People: The Truth About America's Disappearing Jobs and Why Universal Basic Income Is Our Future*, Hachette Books; 1 edition (April 3, 2018)

10. Thomas Piketty, *Capital in the Twenty-First Century*, The Belknap Press of Harvard University Press, 2014.

11. Speech before the UN General Assembly, 25 September 2018, https://basicincome.org/news/2018/09/un-secretary-general-endorses-ubi/

Chapter 14: Start with a Pilot Project

1. More information about Blue Ridge Electric Membership Corporation community solar gardens is at https://www.blueridgeenergy.com/residential/powerful-solutions/community-solar. In another example, the Shenandoah Valley Electric Cooperative in Virginia partnered with EDF Renewables North America to deliver solar electricity to its members, https://www.dailyprogress.com/newsvirginian/news/shenandoah-valley-electric-cooperative-co-op-joins-solar-partnership/article_404cdd4a-eda9-5756-940c-9767f71bb962.html

2. The $1,000 per month basic income is in line with the amount suggested by this report: Institute for Alternative Futures. *Human Progress and Human Services 2035: A Scenario Exploration*. Alexandria, VA. September 2018. Available from https://altfutures.org/projects/human-progress-and-human-services-2035/. Also, $1,005/month is suggested by Scott Santens of the Economic Security Project in his paper *How to Reform Welfare and Taxes to Provide Every American Citizen with a Basic Income*, https://medium.com/economicsecproj/how-to-reform-welfare-and-taxes-to-provide-every-american-citizen-with-a-basic-income-bc67d3f4c2b8

3. Aviva Rutkin, *Blockchain-based microgrid gives power to consumers in New York*, New Scientist, 2 March 2016, https://www.newscientist.com/article/2079334-blockchain-based-microgrid-gives-power-to-consumers-in-new-york/

4. Jacob Aron, *SolarCoin cryptocurrency pays you to go green*, New Scientist 6 February 2014, https://www.newscientist.com/article/dn25010-solarcoin-cryptocurrency-pays-you-to-go-green/

5. Mein Grundeinkommen has a website in German https://www.mein-grundeinkommen.de/ and in English https://www.mein-grundeinkommen.de/infos/in-english

6. André Coelho, *Germany: The HartzPlus experiment is starting, and the basic income discussion is there to stay*, March 3, 2019, https://basicincome.org/news/2019/03/germany-the-hartzplus-experiment-is-starting-and-the-basic-income-discussion-is-there-to-stay/

Chapter 15: Conclusion

1. Adrian J. Bradbrook & Judith G. Gardam, "Placing Access to Energy Services within a Human Rights Framework", *Human Rights Quarterly* 28 (2006) 389–415 The Johns Hopkins University Press, https://doi.org/10.1353/hrq.2006.0015

Appendix A: Do The Numbers Add Up?

1. Andrew Yang, *The War on People: The Truth About America's Disappearing Jobs and Why Universal Basic Income Is Our Future*, Hachette Book Group, Inc., 2018.

2. Andy Stern with Lee Kravitz, *Raising the Floor: How a Universal Basic Income Can Renew Our Economy and Rebuild the American Dream*, Public Affairs Publishing, 2016.

3. This capacity factor was derived from the PVWatts Solar Calculator (https://pvwatts.nrel.gov/pvwatts.php) for an array in Seattle tilted up to its latitude of 47 degrees.

4. Wikipedia contributors, "Growth of photovoltaics," Wikipedia, The Free Encyclopedia, https://en.wikipedia.org/wiki/Growth_of_photovoltaics (accessed 12 August 2019).

5. Wikipedia contributors, "List of countries by energy consumption per capita." Wikipedia, The Free Encyclopedia, https://en.wikipedia.org/wiki/List_of_countries_by_energy_consumption_per_capita (accessed 12 August 2019).

6. Wikipedia contributors, "World Energy Consumption," Wikipedia, The Free Encyclopedia, https://en.wikipedia.org/wiki/World_energy_consumption (accessed 13 August 2019).

7. Ram M., Bogdanov D., Aghahosseini A., Gulagi A., Oyewo A.S., Child M., Caldera U., Sadovskaia K., Farfan J., Barbosa LSNS., Fasihi M., Khalili S., Dalheimer B.,Gruber G., Traber T., De Caluwe F., Fell H.-J., Breyer C. *Global Energy System based on 100% Renewable Energy –Power, Heat, Transport and Desalination Sectors*. Study by Lappeenranta University of Technology and Energy Watch Group, Lappeenranta, Berlin,March 2019. http://energywatchgroup.org/wp-content/uploads/EWG_LUT_100RE_All_Sectors_Global_Report_2019.pdf

Notes and References

Additional Resources

Basic Income

Give People Money: How a Universal Basic Income Would End Poverty, Revolutionize Work, and Remake the World by Annie Lowrey, Crown, 2018.

Basic Income: A Radical Proposal for a Free Society and a Sane Economy, by Philippe Van Parijs and Yannick Vanderborght, Harvard University Press, Cambridge, Massachusetts, 2017.

Basic Income: A Guide for the Open-Minded by Guy Standing, Yale University Press, New Haven, Connecticut, 2017.

The Case for Universal Basic Income by Louise Haagh, Polity Press, Cambridge UK, 2019.

Raising The Floor: How a Universal Basic Income Can Renew Our Economy and Rebuild the American Dream by Andy Stern with Lee Kravitz, PublicAffairs, New York, 2016.

With Liberty and Dividends For All: How to Save Our Middle Class When Jobs Don't Pay Enough by Peter Barnes, Perrett-Koehler Publishers, Inc., San Francisco, 2014.

It's Basic Income: The Global Debate edited by Amy Downes and Stewart Lansley, Policy Press, University of Bristol UK, 2018.

Basic Income Earth Network (BIEN), https://basicincome.org

BIEN National and Regional Affiliates list, https://basicincome.org/about-bien/affiliates/

Unconditional Basic Income Europe (UBIE), https://www.ubie.org/

US Basic Income Guarantee, https://usbig.net

GiveDirectly, https://www.givedirectly.org/

Basic Income Today, The UBI News Hub, https://basicincometoday.com.

Renewable Energy

Energy, Justice and Peace: A Reflection on Energy in the Current Context of Development and Environmental Protection by the Pontifical Council for Peace and Justice, Libreria Editrice Vaticana, The Vatican, 2014.

Energy and the Wealth of Nations: Understanding the Biophysical Economy by Charles A. S. Hall and Kent A. Klitgaard, Springer Science+Business Media, LLC, New York, 2012.

Reinventing Fire: Bold Business Solutions for the New Energy Era by Amory B. Lovins and the Rocky Mountain Institute, Chelsea Green Publishing, White River Junction, Vermont, 2011.

Power Shift: From Fossil Energy to Dynamic Solar Power by Robert Stayton, Sandstone Publishing, 2015.

The Solar Foundation, https://thesolarfoundation.org.

The Rocky Mountain Institute, http://rmi.org.

Grid Alternatives, https://gridalternatives.org.

REN21: Renewables Now, https://www.ren21.net/

Union of Concerned Scientists, https://ucsusa.org

Economics

Surviving the Future: Culture, Carnival and Capital in the Aftermath of the Market Economy by David Fleming, Chelsea Green Publishing, White River Junction, Vermont, 2016.

Right Relationship: Building a Whole Earth Economy by Peter G. Brown and Geoff Garver, Berrett-Koehler Publishers, 2009.

The Origin of Wealth: Evolution, Complexity, and the Radical Remaking of Economics by Eric D. Beinhocker, Harvard Business School Press, Boston, Massachusetts, 2006.

The Divide: A Brief Guide to Global Inequality and Its Solutions by Jason Hickel, William Heinemann, London, 2017.

Toxic Inequality: How America's Wealth Gap Destroys Mobility, Deepens the Racial Divide, & Threatens Our Future by Thomas M. Shapiro, Basic Books, New York, 2017.

Factor Five: Transforming the Global Economy through 80% Improvements in Resource Productivity, A Report to the Club of Rome by Ernst von Weiszäcker, Karlson `Charlie' Hargroves, Michael H. Smith, Cheryl Desha and Peter Stasinopoulos, Earthscan, London, 2009.

Cooperatives

California Center for Cooperative Development, https://cccd.coop/

CooperationWorks! The Cooperative Development Network, https://cooperationworks.coop/

Grassroots Economic Organizing, http://www.geo.coop/

Touchstone Energy Cooperatives, https://www.touchstoneenergy.com/

America's Electrical Cooperatives, https://www.electric.coop/

National Cooperative Business Association, https://ncbaclusa.coop/

Cooperatives Europe, https://coopseurope.coop/

National Rural Electrical Cooperative Association, https://www.cooperative.com/nreca/Pages/default.aspx

About the Author

Robert Stayton is a physicist, author, teacher, programmer, inventor, technical writer, typesetter, bread baker, and worm farmer, with one art museum exhibit to his credit. He has degrees in physics and science communication, but not in politics or economics.

His previous book *Power Shift: From Fossil Energy to Dynamic Solar Power* traced the human relationship with energy from the past to the present, and into the future with solar energy. It's one of the few books that explains energy so the average person can understand it.

His first book, published in 2002 and entitled *DocBook XSL: The Complete Guide*, established him as a world expert in DocBook, the open-source software for computer-based publishing used by people and companies around the world. This book was edited and formatted using DocBook.

Index

CPSIA information can be obtained
at www.ICGtesting.com
Printed in the USA
FSHW022043010919
61526FS